Benjamin Wilson

The sacred melodist

Being a collection of Psalms, hymns and spiritual songs

Benjamin Wilson

The sacred melodist

Being a collection of Psalms, hymns and spiritual songs

ISBN/EAN: 9783742863027

Manufactured in Europe, USA, Canada, Australia, Japa

Cover: Foto ©Lupo / pixelio.de

Manufactured and distributed by brebook publishing software (www.brebook.com)

Benjamin Wilson

The sacred melodist

PREFACE.

The following Hymn Book has been compiled to meet the wants of brethren, in various localities, who have often expressed a wish for a better, larger, and more varied collection of Hymns; as well as one which should be wholly scriptural in its character. This desire has been constantly kept in view while preparing the Work. How far the object has been accomplished, the judgment of those who may use it will decide. Purity of scriptural sentiment, beauty of diction, and special adaptation for use, have been strictly regarded in this compilation; and though perfection cannot be claimed for any human production, yet it is hoped, that fewer faults will be found in this Hymn Book, than in any other extant.

The Book has been divided into three parts:—Part I, styled *Psalms*,—consisting of metrical compositions founded on the Book of Psalms; Part II, *Hymns*—composed chiefly of Hymns celebrating the perfections of Jehovah; and Part III, *Songs*—including compositions of a more varied character, and embracing a wider range of subjects. This arrangement gives a distinct feature to the Work, and will enable those who wish to observe the precept of the Apostle,—" Singing with gratitude in your hearts to God in Psalms, and Hymns, and Spiritual Songs,"—to do so in an orderly and proper manner.

The Psalms contained in the first Part are not numbered as they are found in the book of Psalms. The Scriptural Index at the end of the Book will give the proper reference. The Hymns and Songs in the second and Third Parts are each numbered separately.

Let those who generally take the lead in the delightful and solemn duty of singing in our Christian assemblies, be careful to select tunes adapted to the Hymns, and in singing to enunciate each word with distinctness, proper emphasis, and feeling, so that all may be edified. And let those who are usually mute in the Congregation train their voices to melody, so that they may assist in sounding forth "the high praises of God" in a becoming and suitable manner.

To sing the praises of the Lord is one of the most pleasing and sublime exercises of social worship. To sing with "the spirit and the understanding," to "praise the name of God with a song," "to sing of the mercies of the Lord," "to sing of his power and righteousness," and "to abundantly utter the memory of his great goodness," pertain to the Christian even in the present state; and, if properly engaged in, will act as a preparative for joining in that nobler ascription of praise to God and the Lamb, which will be sung in the coming age, by those redeemed to God "out of every kindred, and tongue, and people, and nation."

That the following pages may be found to supply the present wants of our brethren, and be promotive of the glory of God, is the earnest desire of the compiler.

BENJAMIN WILSON.

Geneva, Ill., June, 1860.

PSALMS, HYMNS, & SONGS.

PART I.—PSALMS.

PSALM 1.—L. M.

1 Thrice happy he who shuns the way
 That leads ungodly men astray ;
 Who fears to stand where sinners meet,
 Nor with the scorner takes his seat.

2 The law of God is his delight;
 That cloud by day, that fire by night,
 Shall be his comfort in distress,
 And guide him through life's wilderness.

3 His works shall prosper : he shall be
 A fruitful, fair, unwith'ring tree,
 That, planted where the river flows,
 Nor drought, nor frost, nor mildew knows.

4 Not so the wicked; they are cast
 Like chaff upon the whirlwind's blast;
 In judgment they shall quake for dread,
 Nor with the righteous lift their head.

PSALM 2.—C. M.

1 Attend, O earth, whilst I declare
    God's uncontroll'd decree :
"Thou art my Son, this day, my heir,
"Have I begotten thee.

2 "Ask and receive thy full demands;
"Thine shall the nations be ;
"The utmost limits of the lands
"Shall be possess'd by thee.

3 "Thy threat'ning sceptre thou shalt shake,
"And crush them everywhere,
"As massy bars of iron break
"The potter's brittle ware."

4 Learn then, ye Princes, and give ear
    Ye Judges of the earth ;
Worship the Lord with holy fear,
    Rejoice with awful mirth.

PSALM 3.—C. M.

1 Lord, in the morning thou shalt hear
    My voice ascending high ;
To thee will I direct my pray'r,
    To thee lift up mine eye :

2 Up to the hills, where Christ is gone
    To plead for all his saints,
Presenting at his Father's throne
    Our songs and our complaints.

3 Thou art a God before whose sight
    The wicked shall not stand ;

Sinners shall ne'er be thy delight,
  Nor dwell at thy right hand.

4 But to thy house will I resort,
  To taste thy mercies there;
I will frequent thine holy court,
  And worship in thy fear.

5 The men that love and fear thy name,
  Shall see their hopes fulfill'd;
The mighty God will compass them
  With favor as a shield.

PSALM 4.—7s.

1 LORD, our Lord, how great art thou!
Heaven and earth to bless thee bow:
Thou who writ'st thy praise on high,
Glorious on the spreading sky!

2 Yet, the babe's and suckling's song
Thou hast fill'd with strength so strong,
That the raging foe shall quail,
That th' avenger's arm shall fail.

3 When I see thy heavenly arch,
Moon and stars in radiant march,
Where thy hand their station placed;
Where their path thy fingers traced;

4 What has man, O Lord of all,
That thine eye so low should fall?
Thou his honor'd crown hast given
Just beneath the crowns of heaven:

5 Thou hast taught thy works below
Him their sov'reign chief to know:
Flocks and herds, a countless train;
All that roams the fruitful plain:

6 All that cleaves th' ethereal blue;
All that glides the dark waves through:
Lord our Lord, how great art thou!
Heaven and earth to bless thee bow!

PSALM 5.—L. M.

1 ALMIGHTY Ruler of the skies,
Through the wide earth thy name is spread;
And thine eternal glories rise
O'er all the heavens thy hands have made.

2 Lord, what was man, when made at first,
Adam, the offspring of the dust;
That thou should'st set him and his race
But just below an angel's place?

3 That thou should'st raise his nature so,
And make him lord of all below;
Make every beast and bird submit,
And lay the fishes at his feet?

4 Yes! these, and brighter glories wait,
To crown the second Adam's state!
What honors shall thy Son adorn—
He, who of all things is first-born!

5 See him below the angels made,
See him in dust amongst the dead,
To save a ruin'd world from sin;
But he shall reign with power divine.

6 The world to come, redeem'd from all
    The mis'ries that attend the fall,
  New-made and glorious, shall submit
    At our exalted Savior's feet.

PSALM 6.—C. M.

1 To thee, O Lord, I raise my song,
    Thy wonders I proclaim;
  Thou sov'reign Judge of right and wrong,
    For righteous is thy name.

2 I'll sing thy majesty and grace;
    My God prepares his throne
  To judge the world in righteousness,
    And makes his justice known.

3 Then shall the Lord a refuge prove
    For all the poor opprest;
  To save the people of his love,
    And give the weary rest.

4 The men that know thy name will trust
    In thy abundant grace;
  For thou hast ne'er forsook the just
    Who humbly seek thy face.

5 Sing praises to the righteous Lord,
    Whose throne is Zion's hill,
  Who executes his threat'ned word,
    And doth his grace fulfil.

PSALM 7.—C. M.

1 Lord, shall the wicked still deride
    Thy justice and thy power?

Shall they advance their heads in pride
 And still thy saints devour?

2 Arise, O God, lift up thy hand,
 Attend our humble cry;
No enemy shall dare to stand
 When God ascends on high.

3 Why do the men of malice rage,
 And say, with foolish pride,
"The God of heaven will ne'er engage
 To fight on Zion's side."

4 But thou for ever art our Lord,
 And powerful is thy hand,
As when the heathen felt thy sword,
 And perished from thy land.

5 God will prepare our hearts to pray,
 And bow his ear to hear:
Accept the vows thy children pay,
 And free thy saints from fear.

PSALM 8.—C. M.

1 The Lord is in his holy place;
 And from his throne on high,
He looks upon the human race
 With omnipresent eye.

2 He proves the righteous, marks their path;
 In him the weak are strong;
But violence provokes his wrath;
 The Lord abhorreth wrong.

3 God on the wicked will rain down
    Brimstone, and fire, and snares;
  The gloom and tempest of his frown!
    This portion shall be theirs.

4 The righteous Lord will take delight
    Alone in righteousness;
  The just are pleasing in his sight;
    The humble he will bless.

PSALM 9.—C. M.

1 LORD, who's the happy man that may
    To thy bless'd courts repair?
  Not stranger-like, to visit them,
    But to inhabit there?

2 'Tis he whose ev'ry thought and deed
    By rules of virtue moves:
  Whose gen'rous tongue disdains to speak
    The thing his heart disproves.

3 Who never did a slander forge,
    His neighbor's fame to wound,
  Or harken to a false report,
    By malice whisper'd round.

4 The man who, by this steady course,
    Has happiness insur'd,
  When earth's foundations shake, shall stand,
    By Providence secur'd.

PSALM 10.—C. M.

1 THE Lord before me still I set:
    Since it is so that he

Doth ever stand at my right hand,
  I shall not moved be.

2 Because of this my heart is glad,
    My joy shall be exprest
  E'en by my glory; and my flesh
    In confidence shall rest.

3 Because my soul in grave to dwell
    Shall not be left by thee;
  Nor wilt thou give thine Holy One
    Corruption e'er to see.

4 Thou wilt show me the path of life:
    Of joy there is full store
  Before thy face; at thy right hand
    Are pleasures evermore.

5 Thus in the name of Christ, the Lord,
    The psalmist David sung;
  And Providence fulfils the word
    Of his prophetic tongue.

6 Jesus, whom every saint adores,
    Was crucified and slain;
  Behold, the tomb its prey restores!
    Behold, he lives again!

PSALM 11.—L. M.

1 The spacious firmament on high,
  With all the blue ethereal sky,
  And spangled heavens, a shining frame
  Their great Original proclaim.

2 Th' unwearied sun, from day to day,
  Doth his Creator's power display;
  And publishes to every land
  The work of an Almighty hand.

3 Soon as the evening shades prevail,
  The moon takes up the wondrous tale,
  And nightly to the list'ning earth
  Repeats the story of her birth.

4 While all the stars that round her burn,
  And all the planets in their turn,
  Confirm the tidings as they roll,
  And spread the truth from pole to pole.

5 What though in solemn silence all
  Move round this dark terrestrial ball;
  What though no real voice nor sound,
  Amidst their radiant orbs be found.

6 In reason's ear they all rejoice,
  And utter forth a glorious voice;
  Forever singing as they shine,
  " The hand that made us is divine."

PSALM 12.—L. M.

1 The Lord's converting law is pure;
  The Lord's enlight'ning witness, sure;
  The Lord's enliv'ning precepts, right;
  The Lord's commandment, radiant light;

2 The Lord's clean fear is endless youth;
  The Lord's just judgments, spotless truth;
  Far richer than the golden ore,
  Far sweeter than the honey'd store.

3 Safe with such guides, thy servant treads;
And large rewards their path outspreads:
But who can count what steps may slide?
Oh, cleanse the sins that deepest hide!

4 But chief my suppliant soul restrain
From bolder crime's presumptuous reign:
So, upright shall I walk with thee,
So, guilt's dread blight forever flee.

5 The words that e'er my lips may part,
The thoughts that e'er may stir my heart,
Let none thy holy presence mock,
Lord, my Redeemer and my Rock!

PSALM 13.—C. M.

1 Thy law is perfect, Lord of light,
   Thy testimonies sure;
The statutes of thy realm are right,
   And thy commandments pure.

2 Holy, inviolate thy fear,
   Enduring as thy throne;
Thy judgments, chast'ning or severe,
   Justice and truth alone.

3 Let these, O God, my soul convert,
   And make thy servant wise;
Let these be gladness to my heart,
   The day-spring to mine eyes.

4 By these may I be warn'd betimes:
   Who knows the guile within?
Lord, save me from presumptuous crimes,
   Cleanse me from secret sin.

5 So may the words my lips express,
  The thoughts that throng my mind,
 O Lord, my strength and righteousness,
  With thee acceptance find.

PSALM 14.—L. M.

1 My song of praise, O Lord, shall sound,
 Where ransom'd saints adore around:
 And where thy host in bliss shall bow,
 Shall stand redeem'd my grateful vow.

2 There, the meek suff'rer shall rejoice,
 Feast in thy love, and lift his voice:
 The heart that pray'd in praise shall soar,
 And beat with life that dies no more.

3 Earth's utmost bounds shall hear and turn,
 All tribes and realms thy worship learn;
 For God the Lord all empire owns,
 And rules amid their thousand thrones.

4 All, all shall kneel: the rich of earth
 Shall feast and bow in hallow'd mirth,
 And they who down to dust draw nigh,
 And scarce can stay th' expiring sigh.

5 A seed shall serve him, rising fair;
 The Lord's own name their race shall bear:
 And unborn lines of sire and son
 Shall tell what deeds the Lord hath done.

PSALM 15.—11's.

1 The Lord is my shepherd; I ne'er shall have need;
 He gives me my couch on the green, quiet mead;

He leads me beside the still waters; and brings
His wand'rer to pathways where righteousness springs.

2 And though thro' the valley of death's gloomy shade
Thou call'st me to journey, I am not afraid:
No ill shall befall me, with thee at my side,
Thy crook for my comfort, thy staff for my guide.

3 Thou spread'st me a banquet in eye of my foes;
Thou crown'st me with oil: and my cup overflows:
So, goodness and grace shall my footsteps entwine,
And God's holy dwelling shall ever be mine.

PSALM 16.—7's.

1 To thy pastures fair and large,
Heavenly Shepherd, lead thy charge,
And my couch with tend'rest care
Mid the springing grass prepare.

2 When I faint with summer's heat,
Thou shalt guide my weary feet
To the streams that, still and slow,
Through the verdant meadows flow.

3 Safe the dreary vale I tread,
By the shades of death o'erspread,
With thy rod and staff supplied
As my guardian and my guide.

4 Constant to my latest end,
Thou my footsteps shalt attend;
And wilt give abiding rest,
In the mansions of the blest.

PSALM 17.—L. M.

1 Our Lord is risen from the dead,
Our Jesus is gone up on high;

The powers of hell are captive led,
 Dragg'd to the portals of the sky.

2 There his triumphal chariot waits,
 And angels chant the solemn lay,
"Lift up your heads, ye heavenly gates!
"Ye everlasting doors give way!"

3 Loose all your bars of massy light,
 And wide unfold the radiant scene;
He claims those mansions as his right,
 "Receive the King of glory in."

4 "Who is this King of glory, who?"
 The Lord that all his foes o'ercame,
The world, sin, death, and hell o'erthrew,
 And Jesus is the conqueror's name.

5 Lo! his triumphal chariot waits,
 And angels chant the solemn lay,
"Lift up your heads, ye heavenly gates!
"Ye everlasting doors give way!"

6 "Who is this King of glory, who?"
 The Lord of boundless power possess'd;
He is the King of nations too;
 Lord over all, forever bless'd!

PSALM 18.—C. M.

1 Soon as I heard my Father say,
 "Ye children seek my grace,"
My heart replied without delay,
 "I'll seek my Father's face."

2 Let not thy face be hid from me,
    Nor frown my soul away;
  God of my life, I fly to thee
    In a distressing day.

3 Should friends and kindred, near and dear,
    Leave me to want or die;
  My God would make my life his care,
    And all my need supply.

4 My fainting flesh had died with grief,
    Had not my soul believed,
  That grace would soon provide relief:
    Nor was my hope deceived.

5 Wait on the Lord, ye trembling saints,
    And keep your courage up;
  He'll raise your spirit when it faints,
    And far exceed your hope.

PSALM 19.—C. M.

1 Grant me within thy courts a place,
    Among thy saints a seat,
  For ever to behold thy face
    And worship at thy feet:

2 In thy pavilion to abide,
    When storms of trouble blow;
  And in thy tabernacle hide,
    Secure from every foe.

3 Oh leave me not when griefs assail,
    And earthly comforts flee;
  Should father, mother, kindred fail,
    My God, remember me.

4 Wait on the Lord, with courage wait;
  My soul, disdain to fear:
The righteous Judge is at the gate,
  And thy redemption near.

PSALM 20.—11's.

1 Give glory to God in the highest; give praise,
    Ye noble, ye mighty, with joyful accord;
  All-wise are his counsels, all-perfect his ways,
    In the beauty of holiness worship the Lord.

2 The voice of the Lord on the ocean is known,
    The God of eternity thund'reth abroad;
  The voice of the Lord from the depth of his throne,
    Is terror and power—all nature is awed.

3 At the voice of the Lord, the tall cedars are bow'd,
    And towers from their base into ruin are hurl'd,
  The voice of the Lord from the dark-bosom'd cloud,
    Dissevers the lightning in flames o'er the world.

4 The voice of the Lord through the calm of the wood,
    Awakens its echoes, strikes light thro' the caves;
  The Lord sitteth King on the turbulent flood;
    The winds are his servants, his servants the waves.

5 The Lord is the strength of his people; the Lord
    Gives health to his chosen, and peace evermore:
  Then throng to his temple, his glory record;
    But oh! when he speaketh—in silence adore.

PSALM 21.—S. M.

1 How great thy goodness, Lord,
    Laid up for thine with thee;
  Wrought for the souls that trust thy word;
    That all that live may see!

2 Thy presence holds them safe
    From man's assailing pride:
Though warring tongues around them chafe,
    Within thy tent they hide.

3 The gracious Lord be bless'd,
    My city's tower and wall!
For when, by thronging terrors press'd,
    I fled, and seemed to fall;

4 Then rose my wild complaint,
    "I perish from thine eye!"
But love the Lord, each suppliant saint;
    He heard my doubting cry.

5 The Lord preserves the true,
    And pays the deed of pride:
Stand, and your strength shall he renew,
    Ye that his time abide!

PSALM 22.—C. M.

1 REJOICE, ye righteous, in the Lord:
    This work belongs to you:
Sing of his name, his ways, his word,
    How holy, just, and true.

2 His works of nature and of grace
    Reveal his wondrous name:
His mercy and his righteousness
    Let heaven and earth proclaim.

3 His wisdom and almighty word
    The heavenly arches spread;
And by the spirit of the Lord
    Their shining hosts were made.

4 He made the liquid waters flow
   To their appointed deep:
 The flowing seas their limits know,
   And their own station keep.

5 Ye tenants of the spacious earth,
   With fear before him stand!
 He spoke, and nature took its birth,
   And rests on his command.

6 He scorns the angry nations' rage,
   And breaks their vain designs;
 His counsel stands through every age,
   And in full glory shines.

PSALM 23.—11's & 8's.

Rejoice in the Lord, O ye righteous, rejoice!
  The upright his praises should sing;
With harp and with psalt'ry attune your glad voice,
  And loud let the harmony ring:
Oh sing of his righteousness, sing of his love,
  His judgment and mercy proclaim;
Earth is fill'd with his goodness, while angels above
  Rejoice in his glorious name.

By the word of the Lord the bright heavens were made,
  The earth, the wide waters that roar.
Oh fear him, ye nations, let earth be afraid,
  Stand in awe of his glory and power.
He spake—it was done; he commanded—it rose;
  The universe sprang into view!
His counsels shall stand, though vain mortals oppose,
  His ways are all righteous and true.

How blest is the nation whose God is the Lord,
  The land where in mercy he dwells;
Where thousands rejoice in his worship and word,
  Where wonders of grace he reveals!

Oh trust in his name, in his wisdom confide,
  Nor look to his creatures for aid:
Our souls shall rejoice, while in him we abide,
  Though troubles and sorrows invade.

PSALM 24.—c. m.

1 Through all the changing scenes of life,
    In trouble and in joy,
  The praises of my God shall still
    My heart and tongue employ.

2 Of his deliv'rance I will boast,
    Till all that are distress'd,
  From my example, comfort take,
    And charm their griefs to rest.

3 O! magnify the Lord with me,
    With me exalt his name:
  When in distress to him I call'd,
    He to my rescue came.

4 O make but trial of his love,
    Experience will decide
  How bless'd they are, and only they,
    Who in his truth confide.

5 Fear him, ye saints, and you will then
    Have nothing else to fear;
  Make you his service your delight,
    He'll make your wants his care.

PSALM 25.—l. m.

1 High in the heavens, eternal God,
    Thy goodness in full glory shines;

Thy truth shall break through every cloud
  That veils and darkens thy designs.

2 For ever firm thy justice stands,
    As mountains their foundations keep;
  Wise are the wonders of thy hands;
    Thy judgments are a mighty deep.

3 Thy providence is kind and large,
    Both man and beast thy bounty share;
  The whole creation is thy charge,
    But saints are thy peculiar care.

4 Life, like a fountain rich and free,
    Springs from the presence of the Lord;
  And in thy light our souls shall see
    The glories promised in thy word.

PSALM 26.—S. M.

1 Far as the boundless sky
    Thy mercy, Lord, ascends;
  Far as the rolling clouds can fly,
    Thy sacred truth extends.

2 Strong as th' eternal hills,
    Thy justice holds its sway;
  Deep as the depths old ocean fills,
    Thy judgments' wondrous way.

3 Guard of all living things!
    How precious is thy love,
  That spreads the shadow of its wings
    Our trusting race above!

4 Thy household's fulness sweet
    Shall sate our longing dreams;

And thine own Eden's joyous seat
    Shall pour refreshing streams.

5 For thine is life's pure rill;
    Thine is the light of light:
Oh, give thy saints thy mercy still,
    And give the righteous right.

6 Far be the foot of pride,
    And far the wasting hand;
And lo! the false transgressors slide,
    They fall, they ne'er shall stand!

PSALM 27.—L. M.

1 I WAITED meekly for the Lord,
    Till he vouchsafed a kind reply;
Who did his gracious ear afford,
    And heard from heaven my humble cry.

2 Who can the wond'rous works recount,
    Which thou, O God, for us hast wrought?
The treasures of thy love surmount
    The power of numbers, speech, and thought.

3 I've learnt that thou hast not desired
    Off'rings and sacrifice alone;
Nor blood of guiltless beasts required
    For man's transgression to atone.

4 I therefore come—come to fulfil
    The oracles thy books impart;
'Tis my delight to do thy will;
    Thy law is written on my heart.

PSALM 28.—C. M.

1 How many are thy thoughts of love!
  Thy mercies, Lord, how great!
 We have not words nor hours enough
  Their numbers to repeat.

2 When I'm afflicted, poor and low,
  And light and peace depart;
 My God beholds my heavy woe,
  And bears me on his heart.

3 Thus saith the Lord, "Your work is vain,
  " Give your burnt-offerings o'er,
 " In dying goats and bullocks slain
  " My soul delights no more."

4 Then spoke the Savior, "Lo, I'm here,
  " My God, to do thy will;
 " Whate'er thy sacred books declare,
  " Thy servant shall fulfil.

5 " Thy law is ever in my sight,
  " I keep it near my heart;
 " Mine ears are open'd with delight
  " To what thy lips impart."

PSALM 29.—L. M.

1 God of salvation, we adore
 Thy saving love, thy saving power;
 And to our utmost stretch of thought
 Hail the redemption thou hast wrought.

2 Perish each thought of human pride;
 Let God alone be magnified;

His glory let the heavens resound,
Shouted from earth's remotest bound.

3 Let all who his salvation know,
Saints, who but taste it here below,
Join every angel's voice to raise
Continued, never-ending praise.

PSALM 30.—C. M.

1 As pants the hart for cooling streams,
   When heated in the chase,
So longs my soul, O God, for thee,
   And thy refreshing grace.

2 For thee, my God, the living God,
   My thirsty soul doth pine;
O when shall I behold thy face,
   Thou majesty divine?

3 Why restless, why cast down, my soul?
   Trust God, who will employ
His aid for thee, and change these sighs
   To thankful hymns of joy.

4 Why restless, why cast down, my soul?
   Hope still, and thou shalt sing
The praise of him who is thy God,
   Thy health's eternal spring.

PSALM 31.—L. M.

1 Now be my heart inspired to sing
The glories of my Savior-King:
Jesus the Lord, his form how fair!
How rich, how bright his beauties are.

2 O'er all the sons of human race
  He shines with majesty and grace;
  Love from his lips divinely flows,
  And blessings all his state compose.

3 Dress thee in arms, Almighty Lord!
  Gird on the terrors of thy sword!
  In majesty and glory ride,
  With truth and meekness at thy side.

4 Thine anger, like a pointed dart,
  Shall pierce the foes of stubborn heart;
  Or words of mercy, kind and sweet,
  Shall melt the rebels at thy feet.

5 Thy throne, O God, forever stands,
  Grace is the sceptre in thy hands;
  Thy laws are just, thy judgments right,
  Justice and grace are thy delight.

6 God, thy own God, hath richly shed
  His oil of gladness on thy head;
  And with his sacred spirit blest
  His first-born Son above the rest.

PSALM 32.—P. M.

1 God is our refuge in distress,
  A present help when dangers press;
    In him undaunted we'll confide;
  Though earth were from her centre tost,
  And mountains in the ocean lost,
    Torn piecemeal by the roaring tide.

2 A gentler stream with gladness still
  The City of our Lord shall fill,
    The royal seat of God most high:

God dwells in Zion, whose fair towers
Shall mock the assault of earthly powers,
   While his almighty aid is nigh.

3 Submit to God's almighty sway,
   For him the nations shall obey,
      And earth her Sov'reign Lord confess;
   The God of Hosts is strong in arms,
   Our tow'r of refuge in alarms,
      As to our fathers in distress.

PSALM 33.—L. M.

1 O ALL ye nations, clap your hands,
      And let your shouts of vict'ry ring,
   To praise the Lord of all your lands,
      The broad creation's awful King.

2 He treads the realms beneath our feet,
      He breaks the hostile armies down,
   And gives and guards his chosen seat,
      The home of Jacob's old renown.

3 God is gone up with shouting throngs;
      Before him peal'd the trumpet's call:
   Oh, sing to God with lofty songs;
      Sing praises to the Lord of all!

4 Oh, sing to God a royal strain,
      To earth's high King a raptur'd cry:
   God o'er the nations spreads his reign,
      God lifts his holy seat on high.

5 The heirs of many a Gentile throne
      With God's and Abraham's seed adore:
   The shields of earth are all his own,
      And high as heaven his glories soar.

PSALM 34.—C. M.

1 Throned on a cloud our God shall come,
    Bright flames prepare his way,
  Thunder and darkness, fire and storm,
    Lead on the dreadful day.

2 Heaven from above his call shall hear,
    Attending angels come,
  And earth and hell shall know and fear
    His justice and their doom.

3 "But gather all my saints," he cries,
    "That made their peace with God
  "By the Redeemer's sacrifice,
    "And seal'd it with his blood.

4 "Their faith and works brought forth to light,
    "Shall make the world confess
  "My sentence of reward is right,
    "And heaven adore my grace."

PSALM 35.—L. M.

1 Be thou exalted, O my God,
    Above the heavens where angels dwell,
  Thy power on earth be known abroad,
    And land to land thy wonders tell.

2 My heart is fix'd; my song shall raise
    Immortal honors to thy name;
  Awake, my tongue, to sound his praise,
    My tongue, the glory of my frame.

3 High o'er the earth his mercy reigns,
    And reaches to the utmost sky;

His truth to endless years remains,
    When lower worlds dissolve and die.

4 Be thou exalted, O my God,
    Above the heavens where angels dwell,
Thy power on earth be known abroad,
    And land to land thy wonders tell.

PSALM 36.—S. M.

1   When, overwhelm'd with grief,
        My heart within me dies,
    Hopeless, and far from all relief,
        To heaven I lift mine eyes.

2   Oh lead me to the rock
        That's high above my head,
    And make the covert of thy wings
        My shelter and my shade.

3   Within thy presence, Lord,
        Forever I'll abide;
    Thou art the tower of my defence,
        The refuge where I hide.

4   Thou givest me the lot
        Of those that fear thy name;
    If endless life be their reward,
        I shall possess the same.

PSALM 37.—C. M.

1 Early my God, without delay,
    I haste to seek thy face;
My thirsty spirit faints away,
    Without thy cheering grace.

2 So pilgrims on the scorching sand,
   Beneath a burning sky,
 Long for a cooling stream at hand;
   And they must drink or die.

3 I've seen thy glory and thy power
   Through all thy temple shine;
 My God, repeat that heavenly hour,
   That vision so divine.

4 Not life itself with all its joys
   Can my best passions move,
 Or raise so high my cheerful voice,
   As thy forgiving love.

5 Thus till my last expiring day
   I'll bless my God and King;
 Thus will I lift my hands to pray,
   And tune my lips to sing.

PSALM 38.—L. M.

1 GREAT God, indulge my humble claim,
   Thou art my hope, my joy, my rest;
 The glories that compose thy name
   Stand all engaged to make me blest.

2 Thou great and good, thou just and wise,
   Thou art my Father, and my God;
 And I am thine by sacred ties,
   Thy Son, thy servant, bought with blood.

3 With heart, and eyes, and lifted hands,
   For thee I long, to thee I look;
 As travellers in thirsty lands
   Pant for the cooling water brook.

4 With early feet I love t' appear
   Among thy saints and seek thy face;
 Oft have I seen thy glory there,
   And felt the power of sovereign grace.

5 I'll lift my hands, I'll lift my voice,
   While I have breath to pray or praise;
 This work shall make my heart rejoice,
   And spend the remnant of my days.

PSALM 39.—L. M.

1 At God's command the morning ray
 Smiles in the east and leads the day;
 Seasons and times obey his voice,
 The evening and the morn rejoice.

2 'Tis from his watery stores on high
 He gives the thirsty ground supply:
 The yielding earth, made soft with showers
 Dresses herself with plants and flowers.

3 The desert grows a fruitful field,
 Abundant food the valleys yield;
 The plains lift up their cheerful voice,
 The hills repeat th' echoing joys.

4 Thy works pronounce thy power divine,
 O'er every field thy glories shine;
 Through every month thy gifts appear;
 Great God, thy goodness crowns the year.

PSALM 40.—C. M.

1 Shine, mighty God, on Zion shine,
   With beams of heavenly grace;

Reveal thy power through all the land,
  And show thy smiling face.

2 When shall thy name from shore to shore
    Sound through the earth abroad,
  And distant nations know and love
    Their Savior and their God?

3 Sing to the Lord, ye distant lands,
    Sing loud with solemn voice;
  Let every tongue exalt his praise,
    And every heart rejoice.

4 Earth shall obey his high command,
    And yield her full increase;
  And God will crown each chosen land
    With fruitfulness and peace.

PSALM 41.—S. M.

1 To bless thy chosen race,
    In mercy, Lord, incline,
  And cause the brightness of thy face
    On all thy saints to shine.

2 That so thy wond'rous ways
    May through the world be known,
  Whilst distant lands their tribute pay,
    And thy salvation own.

3 Let diff'ring nations join
    To celebrate thy fame,
  Let all the world, O Lord, combine
    To praise thy glorious name.

4 Oh let them shout and sing
    With joy and pious mirth,
  For thou, the righteous judge and king,
    Shalt govern all the earth.

PSALM 42.—L. M.

1 God grant us blessings, grant us grace,
  And lift the brightness of thy face;
  Till all the world thy ways shall know,
  The realms to thy salvation flow.

2 Thy praise, O God, let nations raise,
  Let all the nations hymn thy praise;
  And one high song of gladness soar
  From ev'ry tribe of ev'ry shore.

3 For thou shalt judge the world in right,
  And lead the people by thy might:
  Thy praise, O God, let nations raise,
  Let all the nations hymn thy praise.

4 So earth shall yield her large increase,
  And God, our God, shall send us peace:
  Our homes shall taste his blessing here,
  And earth's far bounds shall learn his fear.

PSALM 43.—L. M.

1 Let God arise in all his might,
  To put his enemies to flight,
  As smoke that sought to cloud the skies
  Before the rising tempest flies.

2 He comes! array'd in burning flames;
  Justice and vengeance are his names:
  Behold his fainting foes expire,
  Like melting wax before the fire.

3 He rides and thunders thro' the sky;
  His name JEHOVAH sounds on high:
  Sing to his name, ye sons of grace;
  Ye saints, rejoice before his face.

4 The widow and the fatherless,
  Fly to his aid in sharp distress;
  In him the poor and helpless find,
  A Judge that's just, a Father kind.

5 He breaks the captive's heavy chain,
  And prisoners see the light again;
  But rebels that dispute his will,
  Shall dwell in chains and darkness still.

PSALM 44.—L. M.

1 KINGDOMS and thrones to God belong;
  Crown him, ye nations, in your song;
  His wondrous names and powers rehearse,
  His honors shall enrich your verse.

2 He shakes the heavens with loud alarms!
  How terrible is God in arms!
  In Israel are his mercies known,
  Israel is his peculiar throne.

3 Proclaim him King, pronounce him blest;
  He's your defence, your joy, your rest:
  When terrors rise, and nations faint,
  God is the strength of every saint.

PSALM 45.—C. M.

1 FATHER! we sing thy wondrous grace,
  We bless our Savior's name,

He bought salvation for the poor,
  And bore the sinner's shame.

2 His dying groans, his living songs,
    Shall better please our God,
  Than harp or trumpet's solemn sound,
    Than goat's or bullock's blood.

3 This shall his humble followers see,
    And set their hearts at rest;
  They by his death draw near to thee,
    And live for ever blest.

4 Let heaven, and all that dwell on high,
    To God their voices raise,
  While land and seas assist the sky,
    And join t'advance the praise.

5 Zion is thine, most holy God,
    Thy Son shall bless her gates;
  And glory purchased by his blood,
    For thine own Israel waits.

PSALM 46.—L. M.

1 Great God! whose universal sway
  The known and unknown worlds obey;
  Now give the kingdom to thy Son,
  Extend his power, exalt his throne.

2 The sceptre well becomes his hands;
  E'en kings shall bow to his commands;
  His justice shall avenge the poor,
  And pride and rage prevail no more.

3 With power he vindicates the just,
  And treads th' oppressor in the dust;

His worship and his fear shall last
Till hours and years and time be past.

4 The saints shall flourish in his days,
Drest in the robes of joy and praise,
Peace like a river from his throne,
Shall flow to nations yet unknown.

PSALM 47.—L. M.

1 Jesus shall reign where'er the sun
Doth his successive journeys run;
His kingdom stretch from shore to shore,
Till moons shall wax and wane no more.

2 For him shall endless prayer be made,
And princes throng to crown his head;
His name like sweet perfume shall rise
With every morning sacrifice;

3 People and realms of every tongue
Dwell on his love with sweetest song;
And infant voices shall proclaim
Their early blessings on his name.

4 Blessings abound where'er he reigns,
The pris'ner leaps to lose his chains;
The weary find eternal rest,
And all the sons of want are blest.

5 Where he displays his healing power,
Death and the curse are known no more;
In him the tribes of Adam boast
More blessings than their father lost.

6 Let every creature rise and bring
Peculiar honors to our King;

Angels descend with songs again,
And earth repeat the loud Amen.

PSALM 48.—7s.

1 HASTEN, Lord, the glorious time,
  When, beneath Messiah's sway,
Every nation, every clime,
  Shall the gospel call obey.

2 Highest kings his power shall own,
  Heathen tribes his name adore;
Satan and his host o'erthrown,
  Bound in chains, shall hurt no more.

3 Then shall wars and tumults cease,
  Then be banish'd grief and pain;
Righteousness, and joy and peace,
  Undisturb'd shall ever reign.

4 Bless we then our gracious Lord,
  Ever praise his glorious name;
All his mighty acts record,
  All his wondrous love proclaim.

PSALM 49.—7's & 6's.

1 HAIL to the Lord's anointed,
  Great David's greater Son;
Hail in the time appointed,
  His reign on earth begun!
He comes to break oppression,
  To set the captive free,
To take away transgression,
  And rule in equity.

2 He comes with succor speedy
    To those who suffer wrong;
To help the poor and needy,
    And bid the weak be strong;
To give them songs for sighing,
    Their darkness turn to light,
Whose souls, condemn'd and dying,
    Were precious in his sight.

3 He shall come down like showers
    Upon the fruitful earth:
And love and joy, like flowers,
    Spring in his path to birth;
Before him on the mountains,
    Shall peace, the herald, go;
And righteousness, in fountains,
    From hill to valley flow.

4 For him shall prayer unceasing
    And daily vows ascend;
His kingdom still increasing
    A kingdom without end:
The tide of time shall never
    His covenant remove;
His name shall stand for ever—
    That name to us is LOVE.

PSALM 50.—C. M.

1 GIVE, Lord, the king, the kingly heir,
    Thy sceptre and thy rod:
So shall the meek his justice share,
    The people of our God.

2 The mountains' sides with peace shall wave,
    And truth the hills shall crown;

His arm the sons of want shall save,
  And break th' oppressor down.

3 Long as the sun shall mount in light,
  Or moons shall wax and wane,
 While age by age sweeps on its flight,
  Shall mortals fear thy reign.

4 All monarchs at his feet shall bow,
  All realms shall be his land;
 For he shall hear the suff'rer's vow,
  And help the helpless hand.

5 His grace the humble shall redeem
  From hostile fraud and strife;
 And precious in his high esteem
  Shall be their guarded life.

6 His name shall stand, when last the sun
  Shall tinge the purple West;
 And ev'ry kingdom, link'd in one,
  Shall bless him, and be bless'd.

7 Forever prais'd be God the Lord,
  Our Israel's Savior strong:
 Let all the earth his name record,
  His glorious praise prolong!

PSALM 51.—L. M.

1 How long, O God, shall hate revile?
 How long thy foes blaspheming smile?
 Why lies thy arm'd right hand in rest?
 Oh, pluck it from thy sheathing breast!

2 Think on the people thou hast bought,
  The tribes thine arm from bondage brought;

Think on Mount Zion's chosen halls,
And turn thee tow'rds their wasted walls.

3 The foe's bold feet profane thy soil;
Thy foes rush in with crime and spoil:
They shout within thy place of pray'r,
And lift their conqu'ring standards there.

4 Remember, Lord, th' opposers' crowd,
The fools' blasphemings, bold and loud:
Forsake not thou thy mourning dove,
But shield the people of thy love.

5 Think on the cov'nant: ev'ry clime
Sees the dark holds of cruel crime;
Oh, turn not back th' oppress'd with shame;
Let want and woe extol thy name.

6 Arise, O God, thy cause maintain;
Think on the fools' blaspheming train;
Forget thou not their guilty cry;
Each day, each hour, it swells on high!

PSALM 52.—C. M.

1 In Judah God of old was known,
  His name in Israel great;
In Salem stood his holy throne,
  And Zion was his seat.

2 Among the praises of his saints
  His dwelling-place he chose;
And listen'd to their just complaints
  Against their haughty foes.

3 At thy rebuke, O Jacob's God,
  What powers and empires fell!

Who knows the terrors of thy rod?
  Thy vengeance who can tell?

4 What power can stand before thy sight
    When once thy wrath appears?
  When heaven shines round with dreadful light,
    The earth adores and fears.

5 When God in his own sovereign ways
    Comes down to save th' opprest,
  The wrath of man shall work his praise,
    And he'll restrain the rest.

PSALM 53.—L. M.

1 LORD, when thy vine in Canaan grew,
Thou wast its strength and glory too,
Attack'd in vain by all its foes,
Till the fair Branch of Promise rose.

2 Fair Branch! ordained of old to shoot
From David's stock, from Jacob's root;
Himself a noble vine, and we
Engrafted branches to the tree.

3 'Tis thine own Son, and he shall stand,
Girt with thy strength at thy right hand;
Thy first-born Son, adorn'd and blest
With power and grace above the rest.

PSALM 54.—L. M.

1 GREAT God, attend, while Zion sings
The joy that from thy presence springs:
To spend one day with thee on earth,
Exceeds a thousand days of mirth.

2 Might I enjoy the meanest place
 Within thy house, O God of grace,
 Not tents of ease nor thrones of power
 Should tempt my feet to leave thy door.

3 God is our sun—he makes our day;
 God is our shield—he guards our way:
 From all th' assaults of hell and sin,
 From foes without and foes within.

4 All needful grace will God bestow,
 And crown that grace with glory too;
 He gives us all things, and withholds
 No real good from upright souls.

5 O God, our King, thy sovereign sway
 The glorious hosts of heaven obey;
 While rebels at thy presence flee:
 Blest is the man who trusts in thee.

PSALM 55.—C. M.

1 O Lord of hosts, my King and God,
  How bless'd are they who dwell
 Within the courts thy saints have trod,
  And all thy glory tell!

2 How bless'd are they, whose strength thou art;
  Whose lips but sing thy praise;
 Who bear, within their inmost heart,
  The mem'ry of thy ways!

3 From strength to strength ascend their feet,
  And brighter joys are near;
 Till all, in Zion's holy seat,
  Before our God appear.

4 I love the threshold at the gate
    Where dwells my God within:
More dear to me, e'en there to wait,
    Than rule the tents of sin.

5 For God the Lord, our Sun and Shield,
    Shall grace and glory shed,
Nor one kind gift disdain to yield,
    Where upright spirits tread.

6 O God of hosts, the mighty Lord,
    How richly bless'd is he,
Whose hope shall bring its sure reward,
    Forever fix'd on thee!

PSALM 56.—C. M.

1 Oh, give us, Lord, thy grace to see,
    Thy full salvation give;
Turn thou to us, that, glad in thee,
    Thy people's heart may live.

2 I hearken for the Lord's dear voice,
    And hear him gently say
Peace to the people of his choice,
    Who turn no more astray.

3 Oh, o'er the hearts that fear his name
    His bright salvation glows;
So guards the Lord, in peaceful fame,
    Our smiling land's repose.

4 And truth and mercy joy to meet,
    And justice clings to love:
They bloom like flow'rs beneath our feet,
    They shine, like stars, above.

5 God gives his grace, and o'er the land
   The waving harvests spread :
Beneath his smile the righteous stand,
   And he shall guide their tread.

PSALM 57.—C. M.

1 Among the princes, earthly gods,
   There's none hath power divine ;
Nor is their nature, mighty Lord,
   Nor are their works, like thine.

2 The nations thou hast made shall bring
   Their off'rings round thy throne ;
For thou alone dost wondrous things,
   And thou art God alone.

3 Lord, I would walk with holy feet,
   Teach me thy heavenly ways,
And all my wand'ring thoughts unite
   In God my Father's praise.

PSALM 58.—8's & 7's.

1 Glorious things of thee are spoken,
   Zion, city of our God ;
He whose word can ne'er be broken
   Chose thee for his own abode.
On the Rock of Ages founded,
   Who can shake her sure repose ?
With salvation's wall surrounded,
   She can smile at all her foes.

2 See the streams of living waters,
   Springing from eternal love ;
Well supply her sons and daughters,
   And the fear of want remove :

Who can faint while such a river
    Onward flows her thirst t' assuage—
Grace, which like the Lord, the giver,
    Never fails from age to age?

3 Round each habitation hov'ring,
    See the cloud and fire appear,
For a glory and a cov'ring,
    Showing that the Lord is near!
Glorious things of thee are spoken,
    Zion, city of our God;
He whose word can ne'er be broken
    Forms thee for his own abode.

PSALM 59.—L. M.

1 Thou God, before whose heav'nly state
    Thy saints in sacred rev'rence bow,
Lord God of Hosts, oh, who is great,
    Or who enrob'd with truth, as thou?

2 Thou rul'st the angry ocean's tide,
    And bidd'st its swelling waves repose:
Thou tramplest down the hosts of pride,
    And strew'st afar thy broken foes.

3 The heav'ns are thine, and thine the earth;
    Thou fram'd'st the land, and thou the sea:
Thou gav'st the North and South their birth,
    Tabor and Hermon shout to thee.

4 Thine arm has empire all its own;
    High holds thy strong right hand its sway:
Justice and judgment rear thy throne,
    And truth and grace prepare thy way.

5 How bless'd to know thy trumpet's voice,
  And walk beneath thy guiding eye!
Each day in thee shall such rejoice,
  And thy just pow'r shall lift them high.

PSALM 60.—C. M.

1 Blest are the souls that hear and know
    The gospel's joyful sound;
  Peace shall attend the path they go
    And light their steps surround.

2 Their joy shall bear their spirits up,
    Through their Redeemer's name;
  His righteousness exalts their hope,
    And fills their foes with shame.

3 The Lord, our glory and defence,
    Strength and salvation gives:
  Israel, thy King for ever reigns.
    Thy God forever lives.

PSALM 61.—L. M.

1 Through every age, eternal God,
  Thou art our rest, our safe abode,
  High was thy throne ere heaven was made,
  Or earth, thy humble footstool, laid.

2 Long hadst thou reign'd ere time began,
  Or dust was fashion'd into man;
  And long thy kingdom shall endure
  When earth and time shall be no more.

3 But man, weak man, is born to die,
  Made up of guilt and vanity;
  Thy dreadful sentence, Lord, was just—
  " Return, ye sinners, to your dust!"

4 Death, like an overflowing stream,
Sweeps us away; our life's a dream—
An empty tale—a morning flower,
Cut down and wither'd in an hour.

5 Teach us, O Lord, how frail is man,
And kindly lengthen out our span,
Till, saved from sin, we all may rest,
And be with Christ forever blest.

PSALM 62.—C. M.

1 O God! our help in ages past,
　Our hope for years to come,
Our shelter from the stormy blast,
　And our eternal home.

2 Beneath the shadow of thy throne
　Thy saints have dwelt secure;
Sufficient is thy arm alone,
　And our defence is sure.

3 Before the hills in order stood,
　Or earth received her frame,
From everlasting thou art God,
　To endless years the same.

4 A thousand ages in thy sight
　Are like an evening gone;
Short as the watch that ends the night,
　Before the rising sun.

5 O God, our help in ages past,
　Our hope for years to come;
Be thou our guide while life shall last,
　To our eternal home.

PSALM 63.—L. M.

1 Sweet is the work, my God, my King,
  To praise thy name, give thanks and sing;
  To show thy love by morning light,
  And talk of all thy truth at night.

2 Sweet is the day of sacred rest,
  No mortal care shall seize my breast;
  Oh let my heart in tune be found,
  Like David's harp of solemn sound.

3 My heart shall triumph in my Lord,
  And bless his works, and bless his word;
  Thy works of grace, how bright they shine!
  How deep thy counsels! how divine!

4 Fools never raise their thoughts so high,
  Like brutes they live, like brutes they die;
  Like grass they flourish, till thy breath
  Blasts them in everlasting death.

5 But I shall share a glorious part
  When grace hath well refined my heart,
  And fresh supplies of joy are shed,
  Like holy oil, to cheer my head.

PSALM 64.—L. M.

1 Lord, 'tis a pleasant thing to stand
  In gardens planted by thine hand;
  Let me within thy courts be seen,
  Like a young cedar, fresh and green.

2 There grow thy saints in faith and love,
  Blest with thine influence from above;
  Not Lebanon, with all its trees,
  Yields such a comely sight as these.

3 The plants of grace shall ever live;
 Nature decays, but grace must thrive;
 Time, that doth all things else impair,
 Still makes them flourish strong and fair.

4 Laden with fruits of age, they show
 The Lord is holy, just, and true;
 None that attend his gates shall find
 A God unfaithful or unkind.

PSALM 65.—L. M.

1 With glory clad, with strength array'd,
  The Lord that o'er all nature reigns,
 The world's foundation strongly laid,
  And the vast fabric still sustains.

2 How surely stablish'd is thy throne!
  Which shall no change or period see;
 For thou, O Lord, and thou, alone,
  Art God from all eternity.

3 The floods, O Lord, lift up their voice,
  And toss the troubled waves on high;
 But God above can still their noise,
  And make the angry sea comply.

4 Thy promise, Lord, is ever sure;
  And they that in thy house would dwell,
 That happy station to secure
  Must still in holiness excel.

PSALM 66.—L. M.

1 The Lord is King in realms of light;
  With glory rob'd, on high he reigns:
 The Lord is rob'd with sov'reign might,
  And earth's foundations strong sustains.

2 He fixed the skies, the seas, the lands,
    And naught can change their place or way;
  Thy throne, O Lord, eternal stands,
    Thy years are one unfading day.

3 The floods, O Lord, lift up their voice,
    The mighty floods lift up their roar;
  The floods in tumult loud rejoice,
    And climb in foam the sounding shore.

4 But, mightier than the mighty sea,
    The Lord of glory reigns on high:
  Far o'er its waves we look to thee,
    And see their fury break and die.

5 Thy word is true, thy promise sure,
    That ancient promise, seal'd in love;
  Oh, may thy temple here be pure,
    As thy pure mansions shine above.

PSALM 67.—L. M.

1 O COME, loud anthems let us sing,
  To our salvation's Rock and King;
  Within his gates with psalms rejoice,
  And lift on high our thankful voice.

2 O come, and let our songs accord,
  To bless our God, the only Lord;
  For, high o'er ev'ry worshipp'd throne,
  The Lord our God is Lord alone.

3 The earth's wide bounds are in his hand;
  And by his strength the mountains stand;
  He laid the sea's unfathom'd bed,
  And far the shore's fair landscape spread.

4 Oh, come, and let us lowly fall,
   And on our Maker kneeling call;
   For he is still our God and Rock,
   And we his people and his flock.

5 To-day, to-day, his voice but hear,
   " Oh, close not fast your heart and ear,
   As when of old your fathers' pride
   So long my ling'ring wrath defied.

6 As on their desert march they mov'd,
   My works they saw, mine arm they prov'd;
   And forty years their guilt I bore,
   Till that brief race was seen no more.

7 For thus I spoke and swore in wrath,
   ' They will not choose my holy path;
   Their heart from crime no more will cease,
   They shall not tread my land of peace.' "

PSALM 68.—8's.

1 O COME, let us sing to the Lord,
   In God our salvation rejoice;
  In psalms of thanksgiving record
   His praise, with one spirit and voice:
Jehovah is God, and he reigns
   The God of all gods on his throne;
The strength of the hills he maintains;
   The ends of the earth are his own.

2 O come, let us worship and kneel
   Before our Creator, our God,
  The people who serve him with zeal,
   The sheep who his pastures have trod:

To him let us hearken to-day,—
　The voice that yet speaks from above,—
And all his commandments obey,
　For he that ordain'd them is love.

PSALM 69.—L. M.

Give to the Lord, ye tribes and tongues,
　Give to the Lord his praise and state;
Give to the Lord your sweetest songs,
　And come with gifts, and throng his gate.

Oh, fear and bow in sacred grace,
　And tell each land, that God is King:
He fix'd the world's unchanging base,
　And he its righteous doom shall bring.

Let heaven be glad, let earth rejoice,
　The peopled ocean toss and roar,
The plenteous fields lift high their voice,
　The wood's wild hymn in thunder soar.

So let them hail their sov'reign God;
　For lo, he comes, he comes with might,
To wield the sceptre and the rod,
　To judge the world with truth and right.

PSALM 70.—C. M.

1 Sing to the Lord, ye distant lands,
　Ye tribes of every tongue;
His new discover'd grace demands
　A new and nobler song.

2 Say to the nations, Jesus reigns,
　God's own almighty Son;
His power the sinking world sustains,
　And grace surrounds his throne.

3 Let heaven proclaim the joyful day;
   Joy through the earth be seen;
Let cities shine in bright array,
   And fields in cheerful green.

4 The joyous earth, the bending skies,
   His glorious train display;
Ye mountains sink—ye valleys, rise—
   Prepare the Lord his way.

5 Behold, he comes, he comes to bless
   The nations as their God;
To show the world his righteousness,
   And send his truth abroad.

6 But when his voice shall raise the dead,
   And bid the world draw near,
How will the guilty nations dread
   To see their Judge appear!

PSALM 71.—L. M.

1 Th' Almighty reigns, exalted high
O'er all the earth, o'er all the sky;
Though clouds and darkness veil his feet,
His dwelling is the mercy-seat.

2 Oh ye that love his holy name,
Hate every work of sin and shame;
He guards the soul of all his friends,
And from the snares of hell defends.

3 Immortal light, and joys unknown,
Are for the saints in darkness sown:
Those glorious seeds shall spring and rise,
And the bright harvest bless our eyes.

4 Rejoice, ye righteous, and record
  The sacred honors of the Lord;
  None but the soul that feels his grace
  Can triumph in his holiness.

PSALM 72.—C. M.

1 To our Almighty Maker, God,
    New honors be address'd:
  His great salvation shines abroad
    And makes the nations blest.

2 He spake the word to Abra'm first,
    His truth fulfils the grace;
  The Gentiles make his name their trust,
    And learn his righteousness.

3 Let the whole earth his love proclaim
    With all her diff'rent tongues;
  And spread the honors of his name,
    In rich melodious songs.

PSALM 73.—C. M.

1 Joy to the world, Messiah comes;
    Let earth receive her King;
  Let ev'ry heart prepare him room,
    And heav'n and nature sing.

2 Joy to the earth, the Savior reigns,
    Let men their songs employ,
  While fields, and floods, rocks, hills, and plains,
    Repeat the sounding joy.

3 No more shall fruits refuse to grow,
    Nor thorns infest the ground;
  He comes to make his blessings flow,
    Far as the curse is found.

4 He'll rule the world with truth and grace,
    And make the nations prove,
  The glories of his righteousness,
    And wonders of his love.

PSALM 74.—L. M.

1 The Lord is King, enthroned on high,
    Where radiant cherubs veil the brow;
  Let nations quake beneath his eye,
    Let earth's foundations trembling bow.

2 The Lord is great in Zion's tow'rs,
    And famed above all royal fame;
  Let all thy realms, with all their powers,
    Exalt and dread thy hallowed name.

3 O mighty King, thy sov'reign sway
    The righteous cause has loved and led;
  A law of truth thy tribes obey,
    And judgments just thy glory spread.

4 Exalt the Lord in praises loud,
    And low at God's pure footstool fall;
  So Moses sang, so Aaron bow'd,
    So rose the voice of Samuel's call.

5 Prophets and priests, they called on thee,
    And heard thee from thy cloud in heav'n;
  For firm they kept thy good decree,
    And loved the law thy love had giv'n.

6 Thou heard'st them, Lord, in pard'ning grace,
    Though oft they drew thy chast'ning rod:
  Exalt him in his lofty place,
    For holy reigns the Lord our God!

PSALM 75.—L. M.

1 Before Jehovah's awful throne,
   Ye nations, bow with sacred joy!
Know that the Lord is God alone,
   He can create, and he destroy.

2 His sov'reign power, without our aid,
   Made us of clay, and formed us men;
And when, like wand'ring sheep, we stray'd,
   He brought us to his fold again.

3 We are his people, we his care,
   Our souls and all our mortal frame;
What lasting honors shall we rear,
   Almighty Maker to thy name!

4 We'll crowd thy gates with thankful songs,
   High as the heavens our voices raise;
And earth, with her ten thousand tongues,
   Shall fill thy courts with sounding praise.

5 Wide as the world is thy command;
   Vast as eternity thy love;
Firm as a rock thy truth shall stand,
   When rolling years shall cease to move.

PSALM 76.—L. M.

1 Thy years, O Lord, are still the same;
Age tells to age thine endless name;
And thou shalt yet for Zion rise,
And view her wastes with pitying eyes.

2 Now hastes the time, the time fulfilled;
The Lord his city's walls shall build;
Thy servants watch her prostrate tow'rs,
And love the dust that hides her bow'rs.

3 Then, when her head his Zion rears,
And God's own glorious arm appears,
All kings of earth shall praise thy throne,
All realms shall fear thee, Lord, alone.

4 For God shall hear the humble pray'r,
And make the suff'rer's cause his care;
Till future times his praise record,
And unborn nations bless our Lord.

PSALM 77.—C. M.

1 Let Zion and her sons rejoice,
Behold the promised hour:
Her God hath heard her mourning voice
And comes t' exalt his power.

2 Her dust and ruins that remain
Are precious in our eyes:
Those ruins shall be built again
And all that dust shall rise.

3 The Lord will raise Jerusalem,
And stand in glory there;
Nations shall bow before his name,
And kings attend with fear.

4 He sits a Sovereign on his throne.
With pity in his eyes;
He hears the dying pris'ner's groan,
And sees their sighs arise.

5 He frees the soul condemn'd to death;
Nor, while his saints complain,
Shall it be said, that praying breath
Was ever spent in vain.

PSALM 78.—L. M.

1 O Lord! how just and true thy ways!
How sure thy word! how rich thy grace!
From heav'n thy dwelling place above,
Flow down to us thy gifts of love.

2 As high as thou, above our head,
The starry firmament hast spread;
So far exceeds thy wondrous grace,
Our highest thoughts, our utmost praise.

3 As distant as thy wisdom plac'd,
The rising morning from the west;
So far thou dost our sins remove,
With all a father's pitying love.

4 Thy mercy is for ever sure;
Thy righteousness shall still endure;
Through ev'ry age thy grace shall reign,
And none shall seek thy face in vain.

5 O may our God be ever bless'd,
His name through all the earth confess'd;
And we his saints, in full accord,
Will join to sing, praise ye the Lord.

PSALM 79.—S. M.

1 My soul repeat his praise,
Whose mercies are so great;
Whose anger is so slow to rise,
So ready to abate.

2 High as the heavens are raised
Above the ground we tread,
So far the riches of his grace
Our highest thoughts exceed.

3 His power subdues our sins;
   And his forgiving love,
Far as the east is from the west,
   Doth all our guilt remove.

4 The pity of the Lord,
   To those that fear his name,
Is such as tender parents feel;
   He knows our feeble frame.

5 He knows we are but dust,
   Scatter'd by every breath;
His anger, like a rising wind,
   Can send us swift to death.

6 Our days are as the grass,
   Or like the morning flower:
If one sharp blast sweeps o'er the field,
   It withers in an hour.

7 But thy compassions, Lord,
   To endless years endure;
And children's children ever find
   Thy words of promise sure.

PSALM 80.—L. M.

1 My soul, thy great Creator praise;
When clothed in his celestial rays,
He in full majesty appears,
And like a robe his glory wears.

2 The heavens are for his curtains spread;
Th' unfathom'd deep he makes his bed;
Clouds are his chariot when he flies
On winged storms across the skies.

3 Vast are thy works, Almighty Lord;
  All nature rests upon thy word;
  And the whole race of creatures stand
  Waiting their portion from thy hand.

4 The earth stands trembling at thy stroke,
  And at thy touch the mountains smoke;
  Yet humble souls may see thy face,
  And tell their wants to sovereign grace.

5 In thee my hopes and wishes meet,
  And make my meditation sweet;
  Thy praises shall my breath employ
  Till it expires in endless joy.

PSALM 81.—L. M.

1 O RENDER thanks to God above,
  The Fountain of eternal love,
  Whose mercy firm through ages past
  Has stood, and shall for ever last.

2 Who can his mighty deeds express,
  Not only vast, but numberless!
  What mortal eloquence can raise
  A tribute equal to his praise!

3 Happy are they, and only they,
  Who from thy precepts never stray;
  Who know what's right—nor only so,
  But always practise what they know.

PSALM 82.—C. M.

1 How are thy servants bless'd, O Lord!
    How sure is their defence!
  Eternal wisdom is their guide—
    Their help, Omnipotence.

2 In foreign realms and lands remote,
    Supported by thy care,
  Through burning climes they pass unhurt,
    And breathe in tainted air.

3 When by the dreadful tempest borne
    High on the broken wave,
  They know thou art not slow to hear,
    Nor impotent to save.

4 The storm is laid; the winds retire,
    Obedient to thy will:
  The sea, that roars at thy command,
    At thy command is still.

5 In midst of dangers, fear, and death,
    Thy goodness we'll adore;
  We'll praise thee for thy mercies past,
    And humbly hope for more.

PSALM 83.—C. M.

1 O God, my heart is fully bent
    To magnify thy name;
  My tongue, with cheerful songs of praise,
    Shall celebrate thy fame.

2 To all the list'ning tribes, O Lord,
    Thy wonders I will tell;
  And to those nations sing thy praise,
    That round about us dwell.

3 Because thy mercy's boundless height
    The highest heaven transcends,
  And far beyond th' aspiring clouds
    Thy faithful truth extends.

4 Be thou, O God, exalted high
  Above the starry frame :
And let the world, with one consent,
  Confess thy glorious name.

PSALM 84.—C. M.

1 Jesus, our Lord, ascend thy throne,
  And near thy Father sit;
In Zion shall thy power be known,
  And make thy foes submit.

2 What wonders shall thy gospel do!
  Thy converts shall surpass
The num'rous drops of morning dew,
  And own thy sov'reign grace.

3 God hath pronounced a firm decree,
  Nor changes what he swore—
" Eternal shall thy priesthood be,
  While Aaron's is no more."

4 Jesus, our Priest, for ever lives
  To plead for us above;
Jesus, our King, for ever gives
  The blessings of his love.

5 God shall exalt his glorious head,
  His lofty throne maintain;
Shall strike the powers and princes dead
  Who dare oppose his reign.

PSALM 85.—C. M.

1 Great is the Lord; his works of might
  Demand our noblest songs;
Oh let th' assembled saints unite
  Their harmony of tongues.

2 Great is the mercy of the Lord,
   He gives his children food;
And ever mindful of his word,
   He makes his promise good.

3 His Son, the great Redeemer, came
   To seal his cov'nant sure;
Holy and rev'rend is his name,
   His ways are just and pure.

4 They that would grow divinely wise
   Must with his fear begin:
Our fairest proof of knowledge lies
   In hating every sin.

5 Great is the Lord; his works of might
   Demand our highest praise;
Mercy and truth are his delight,
   And justice marks his ways.

PSALM 86.—C. M.

1 HAPPY is he that fears the Lord,
   And follows his commands;
Who lends the poor without reward,
   Or gives with lib'ral hands.

2 As pity dwells within his breast
   To all the sons of need,
So God shall answer his request
   With blessings on his seed.

3 No evil tidings shall surprise
   His well-establish'd mind;
His soul to God his refuge flies,
   Leaving his fears behind.

4 In times of danger and distress
  Some beams of light shall shine;
For God, his strength and righteousness,
  Shall give him peace divine.

PSALM 87.—7's.

1 PRAISE him with a loud accord,
  Praise him, servants of the Lord!
  Praise him with an endless fame:
  Bless'd for ever be his name!

2 Bless'd while yet the golden sun
  Days and years his course shall run;
  From the Eastern dawning blest,
  To the chambers of the West!

3 Far above the earth and sky,
  Reigns the glorious Lord on high:
  Who so high shall make abode?
  Who is like the Lord our God?

4 Yet he bows to see in love
  Earth below and heav'n above;
  Lifting sorrow from the dust,
  Lifting high the humble just.

5 Such he bids with princes stand,
  With the princes of their land;
  Bids the barren mother's hearth
  Ring with childhood's song of mirth.

PSALM 88.—L. M.

1 NOT to ourselves, who are but dust,
  Not to ourselves is glory due;

But to thy name, thou only just,
   Thou only gracious, wise, and true.

2 The God we serve maintains his throne
   Above the clouds, beyond the skies;
  And may his will on earth be done,
   Supreme, till time and nature dies.

3 Vain are the idols men adore,
   Made by themselves of stone or wood;
  Senseless the mass of glitt'ring ore,
   The silver saint or golden god.

4 Oh Israel! make the Lord thy hope,
   Thy help, thy refuge, and thy rest;
  The Lord shall build thy ruins up,
   And thou shall be for ever blest.

PSALM 89.—L. M.

1 From all that dwell below the skies,
  Let the Creator's praise arise;
  Let the Redeemer's name be sung,
  Through every land, by every tongue.

2 Eternal are thy mercies, Lord,
  Eternal truth attends thy word;
  Thy praise shall sound from shore to shore,
  Till suns shall rise and set no more.

PSALM 90.—7s.

1 All ye nations, praise the Lord,
   All ye lands, your voices raise;
  Heaven and earth, with loud accord,
   Praise the Lord, for ever praise.

2 For his truth and mercy stand,
    Past and present and to be,
  Like the years of his right hand,
    Like his own eternity.

3 Praise him, ye who know his love,
    Praise him from the depths beneath;
  Praise him in the heights above;
    Praise your Maker, all that breathe.

PSALM 91.—C. M.

1 BEHOLD the sure foundation stone!
    Which God in Zion lays,
  To build our heavenly hopes upon,
    And his eternal praise.

2 Chosen of God, for ever dear,
    The saints adore his name;
  They trust their whole salvation here,
    Nor shall they suffer shame.

3 The foolish builders, scribe and priest,
    Reject it with disdain;
  Yet on this Rock the church shall rest,
    And envy rage in vain.

4 What though the gates of hell withstood,
    Yet must this building rise;
  'Tis thine own work, Almighty God,
    And wondrous in our eyes.

PSALM 92.—C. M.

1 BLESS'D be thy name, O Lord my God!
    To me thy laws unfold;

And loud my lips shall tell abroad,
  Whate'er thy lips have told.

2 Beyond the wealth of golden mines,
  Thy precepts are my joy :
The way where thy commandment shines,
  Shall all my cares employ.

3 Folding thy law within my arms,
  I rise in thought above ;
And, musing on its sacred charms,
  My heart o'erflows with love.

4 Bright beams are there, with gladness bright,
  And heavenly raptures flow :
I will not lose the rich delight,
  Which thy pure words bestow.

PSALM 93.—C. M.

1 SACRED and true, O righteous Lord,
  Thy judgments just abide ;
And all thy holy words record,
  Is truth most sure and tried.

2 Righteous and glorious is thy word ;
  My soul shall clasp it still :
Like dawning morn, its beams are pour'd,
  To light the humble will.

3 Priz'd more than gold, than gold, most bright,
  I guard thy words within,
Deem all the Lord's commandments right,
  And shun the paths of sin.

4 Unchang'd as first thy word was pass'd,
  Its quick'ning truths abide ;

And firm thy judgments, Lord, shall last
While endless ages glide.

PSALM 94.—C. M.

1 Long as the rolling years shall glide,
　Or heaven its arch uphold,
Thy promise, Lord, shall firm abide
　Thy truth shall still be told.

2 Low in the depths thy sov'reign hand
　Earth's strong foundations laid;
And all things serve at thy command,
　As all by thee were made.

3 Light, life, and joy thy precepts gave,
　Thy precepts unforgot;
Else deep within the gloomy grave
　Had clos'd my sorrowing lot.

4 Most sweet the words that teach thy will,
　Of all I taste most sweet!
More sweet than honey'd hives distil,
　They guard my tempted feet.

5 No heartless song my lips shall lift,
　To tell my Maker's praise:
Then take, O Lord, their willing gift,
　And teach me all thy ways.

PSALM 95.—C. M.

1 How shall the young secure their hearts
　And guard their lives from sin?
Thy word the choicest rules imparts
　To keep the conscience clean.

2 When once it enters to the mind,
    It spreads such light abroad,
  The meanest souls instruction find,
    And raise their thoughts to God.

3 'Tis like the sun, a heavenly light,
    That guides us all the day;
  And through the dangers of the night,
    A lamp to lead our way.

4 Thy word is everlasting truth,
    How pure is every page!
  That holy book shall guide our youth,
    And well support our age.

PSALM 96.—C. M.

1 LORD, I have made thy word my choice,
    My lasting heritage;
  There shall my noblest powers rejoice,
    My warmest thoughts engage.

2 I'll read the hist'ries of thy love,
    And keep thy laws in sight;
  While through the promises I rove
    With ever new delight.

3 'Tis a broad land of wealth unknown,
    Where springs of life arise;
  Seeds of immortal bliss are sown,
    And hidden glory lies.

4 The best relief that mourners have;
    It makes our sorrows blest:
  Our fairest hope beyond the grave,
    And our eternal rest.

PSALM 97.—C. M.

1 On, pray for Salem's peaceful days!
    And joy for those shall spring,
Who seek thy gates, and love thy praise,
    Thou city of our King!

2 Our feet within thy gates shall climb,
    Thy gates that gleam above;
Thou Salem, thron'd in peace sublime,
    And girt with walls of love!

3 Peace dwell within thy lofty walls,
    And crown thy sacred dome!
And blessings fill the palace halls,
    Our heart's perpetual home!

4 For my lov'd brethren's sake I cry,
    May peace around thee shine!
And for the house of God most High,
    All blessing still be thine!

PSALM 98.—L. M.

1 Who trust the Lord's almighty hand
Like Zion's mount unchang'd shall stand,
Whose rocks forever fast remain,
While storms and foemen dash in vain.

2 As round Mount Zion's sacred charms
The hills extend their circling arms,
So stands the Lord, a host unseen,
His saints' beleagur'd home to screen.

3 Guilt's iron scepter shall not last
Where God his people's lot hath cast,

Nor grow th' oppressor's might so strong,
To bend the upright hand to wrong.

4 Bless, righteous Lord, the righteous heart;
And while the slaves of subtle art,
The tempted share the tempter's doom,
Shall peace and love for Israel bloom.

PSALM 99.—S. M.

1 From lowest depths of woe,
   To God I send my cry:
Lord, hear my supplicating voice,
   And graciously reply.

2 Shouldst thou severely judge,
   Who can the trial bear?
But thou forgiv'st, lest we despond,
   And quite renounce thy fear.

3 My soul with patience waits
   For thee, the living Lord:
My hopes are on thy promise built,
   Thy never-failing word.

4 Let Israel trust in God,
   No bounds his mercy knows;
The plenteous source and spring from whence
   Eternal succor flows.

PSALM 100.—7's.

1 Lord, for ever at thy side
   Let my place and portion be;
Strip me of the robe of pride;
   Clothe me with humility.

2 Meekly may my soul receive
    All thy Spirit hath reveal'd;
Thou hast spoken: I believe,
    Though the prophecy were seal'd.

3 Quiet as a weaned child,
    Weaned from the mother's breast,
By no subtlety beguiled,
    On thy faithful word I rest.

4 Saints, rejoicing evermore,
    In the Lord Jehovah trust;
Him in all his ways adore,
    Wise, and wonderful, and just.

PSALM 101.—L. M.

1 Lord, for thy servant David's sake,
    Perform thine oath to David's Son;
Thy truth thou never wilt forsake;
    Look on thine own Anointed one.

2 The Lord in faithfulness hath sworn
    His throne for ever to maintain;
From realm to realm the sceptre borne,
    Shall stretch o'er earth Messiah's reign.

3 "Zion, my chosen hill of old,
    My rest, my dwelling, my delight,
With loving-kindness I uphold;
    Her walls are ever in my sight.

4 I satisfy her poor with bread,
    Her table in abundance bless;
Joy on her sons and daughters shed,
    And clothe her priests with righteousness."

5 Arise into thy resting place,
    Thou and thy ark of strength, O Lord;
Shine through the veil, we seek thy face—
    Speak, for we hearken to thy word.

PSALM 102.—C. M.

1 BEHOLD, how joyous in the sight,
    How good the spirit's part,
When brethren dear their lot unite,
    One happy home and heart!

2 Not richer once the oil appear'd,
    That, pour'd on Aaron's head,
Flow'd gently down his flowing beard,
    And o'er his garments spread.

3 Not softer dews on Hermon's side
    From balmy skies distil;
Not softer down from heav'n they glide
    To Zion's sacred hill.

4 For there, where love on brethren's breasts
    Has bound its holy tie,
The Lord's eternal blessing rests,
    And life that cannot die.

PSALM 103.—C. M.

1 OH, praise the Lord! With glad acclaim
    The Lord's high honors raise:
Oh, praise the Lord's almighty name;
    Let all that serve him, praise!

2 Oh, praise the Lord! His glory sing,
    All ye that stand and wait
Within the courts of God our King,
    Within his temple gate,

3 Oh, praise the Lord! The Lord is kind,
   The Lord's great name is dear;
In his own Jacob's love enshrin'd,
   In Israel's love and fear.

4 The Lord is great: his great decree
   The wide creation keeps;
The heav'n, the earth, the rolling sea,
   The caverns of the deeps.

5 He lifts the outstretch'd clouds on high,
   And show'r and lightning blends;
And from his treasures in the sky
   The swift-wing'd tempest sends.

6 Thy name, O Lord, endures in light,
   While ages downward flow;
For thou wilt judge thy people's right,
   And pity all their woe.

7 Oh, bless the Lord from Zion's walls,
   The Lord who reigns above,
Yet deigns to dwell in Salem's halls;
   Bless ye the Lord of love.

PSALM 106.—L. M.

1 O RENDER thanks to God above,
The Fountain of eternal love,
Whose mercy firm though ages past
Has stood, and shall for ever last.

2 Who can his mighty deeds express,
Not only vast but numberless!
What mortal eloquence can raise
A tribute equal to his praise!

3 Happy are they, and only they,
Who from thy precepts never stray;
Who know what's right—nor only so,
But always practise what they know.

PSALM 105.—10's.

1 Along the banks where Babel's current flows,
  The captive bands in deep despondence stray'd;
While Zion's fall in sad remembrance rose,
  Her friends, her children, mingled with the dead.

2 The tuneful harp that once with joy they strung,
  When praise employ'd and mirth inspired the lay,
Was now in silence on the willows hung,
  While growing grief prolong'd the tedious day.

3 Their proud oppressors, to increase their woe,
  With taunting smiles a song of Zion claim:
Bid sacred praise in strains melodious flow,
  While they blaspheme the great Jehovah's name.

4 But how, in heathen chains, and lands unknown,
  Shall Israel's bands the sacred anthems raise?
Oh hapless Salem! God's terrestrial throne!
  Thou land of glory, sacred mount of praise!

5 "If e'er my memory lose thy lovely name,
  If my cold heart neglect my kindred race,
Let dire destruction seize this guilty frame,
  My hand shall perish and my voice shall cease.

6 "Yet shall the Lord, who hears when Zion calls,
  O'ertake her foes with terror and dismay,
His arm avenge her desolated walls,
  And bless her children with a peaceful day."

PSALM 106.—L. M.

1 Lord, thou hast search'd and seen me through;
Thine eye commands, with piercing view
My rising and my resting hours,
My heart and flesh, with all their powers.

2 My thoughts before they are my own,
   Are to my God distinctly known;
   He knows the words I mean to speak
   Ere from my opening lips they break.

3 Within thy circling power I stand,
   On every side I find thy hand:
   Awake, asleep, at home, abroad,
   I am surrounded still with God.

4 Amazing knowledge, vast and great!
   What large extent! what lofty height!
   My soul, with all the powers I boast,
   Is in the boundless prospect lost.

5 Oh may these thoughts possess my breast,
   Where'er I rove, where'er I rest;
   Nor let my weaker passions dare
   Consent to sin, for God is there.

PSALM 107.—L. M.

1 Lord, let my prayer like incense rise;
   And when I lift my hands to thee,
   As in the evening sacrifice,
   Look down from heaven well-pleased on me.

2 Set thou a watch to keep my tongue,
   Let not my heart to sin incline;
   Save me from men who practise wrong;
   Let me not share their mirth and wine.

3 But let the righteous, when I stray,
   Smite me in love; his strokes are kind:
   His mild reproofs, like oil, allay
   The wounds they make, and heal the mind.

4 But oh redeem me from the snares
　　With which the world surrounds my feet—
　Its riches, vanities, and cares,
　　Its love, its hatred, and deceit!

PSALM 108.—L. M.

1 My God, my King, thy various praise
　Shall fill the remnant of my days;
　Thy grace employ my humble tongue,
　Till death and glory raise the song.

2 The wings of every hour shall bear
　Some thankful tribute to thine ear:
　And every setting sun shall see
　New works of duty done for thee.

3 Thy works with boundless glory shine,
　And speak thy majesty divine;
　Let every realm with joy proclaim
　The honors of thy holy name.

4 Let distant times and nations raise
　The long succession of thy praise;
　And unborn ages make my song
　The joy and triumph of their tongue.

5 But who can speak thy wondrous deeds?
　Thy greatness all our thoughts exceeds:
　Vast and unsearchable thy ways!
　Vast and immortal be thy praise.

PSALM 109.—L. M.

1 Praise ye the Lord—my heart shall join
　In work so pleasant, so divine;
　My days of praise shall ne'er be past,
　While life, and thought, and being last.

2 Happy the man, whose hopes rely
On Israel's God—he made the sky,
And earth, and seas, with all their train,
And none shall find his promise vain.

3 His truth forever stands secure;
He saves th' oppress'd—he feeds the poor,
He helps the stranger in distress,
The widow and the fatherless.

4 He loves the saints—they are his joy,
But wicked men will he destroy:
Thy God, O Zion, ever reigns;
Praise him in everlasting strains.

PSALM 110.—L. M. 6 lines.

1 I'll praise my Maker with my breath;
And when I'm victor over death,
Praise shall employ my nobler pow'rs:
My days of praise shall ne'er be past,
While life, and thought, and being last,
Or immortality endures.

2 Happy the man, whose hopes rely
On Israel's God;—he made the sky,
And earth and seas, with all their train:
His truth forever stands secure;
He saves th' oppressed, he feeds the poor;
And none shall find his promise vain.

3 I'll praise him while he lends me breath,
And when I'm victor over death,
Praise shall employ my nobler powers;
My days of praise shall ne'er be past,
While life, and thought and being last,
Or immortality endures.

PSALM 111.—L. M.

1 To God loud hallelujahs raise,
Far as his matchless glories shine;
Let heav'n begin and lead the praise,
And universal nature join.

2 The Lord! how absolute he reigns!
Let every angel bend the knee;
Sing of his love in heav'nly strains,
And speak how fierce his terrors be.

3 Wide as his vast dominion lies,
Make the Creator's name be known:
Loud as his thunder shout his praise,
And sound it lofty as his throne.

4 Jehovah's name deserves your praise,
O may it dwell on every tongue!
But saints who best have known his grace,
Are bound to raise the noblest song.

5 Speak of the wonders of that love,
Which Gabriel plays on ev'ry chord:
From all below, and all above,
Loud hallelujahs to the Lord.

PSALM 112.—8's & 7's.

1 PRAISE to thee, thou great Creator!
Praise be thine from every tongue;
Join, my soul, with ev'ry creature,
Join the universal song.

2 Father! Source of all compassion!
Pure, unbounded grace is thine:

Praise the God of our salvation;
 Praise him for his love divine.

3 For ten thousand blessings given,
 For the hope of future joy,
Sound his praise thro' earth and heaven,
 Sound Jehovah's praise on high.

PSALM 113.—10's & 11's.

1 O praise ye the Lord, prepare your glad voice,
 His praise in the great assembly to sing;
In their great Creator let all men rejoice,
 And heirs of salvation be glad in their King.

2 Let them his great name devoutly adore;
 In loud swelling strains his praises express,
Who graciously opens his bountiful store,
 Their wants to relieve, and his children to bless.

2 With glory adorn'd his people shall sing,
 To God, who defence and plenty supplies;
Their loud acclamations to him their great King,
 Thro' earth shall be sounded and reach to the skies.

PSALM 114.—L. M.

1 Praise ye the Lord! yet loftier lays
 With his assembled people sing:
Let Israel tell his Maker's praise.
 And Zion's children bless their King.

2 Oh, praise his name with harp and voice,
 With timbrel's clang, and measur'd tread;
He loves the people of his choice,
 And wreathes with joy the humble head.

3 Oh, let his honor'd saints be strong,
 And sing and slumber undismay'd;

To God's high praise attune the song,
   And grasp with might the conqu'ring blade.

4 So let them quell the broad domains
   Where Gentile darkness hung till now;
And bind their kings with iron chains,
   Their chiefs in lowly fetters bow:

5 So let them bear th' avenging rod
   And do his word's own just award:
Such glory waits the saints of God,
   Through distant years: oh, praise the Lord!

PSALM 115.—7's.

1 PRAISE the Lord, his power confess,
Praise him in his holiness,
Praise him as the theme inspires,
Praise him as his name requires.

2 Let the trumpet's lofty sound
Spread its loudest notes around;
Let the harp unite in praise
With the sacred minstrel's lays.

3 Let the organ join to bless
God, the Lord of righteousness;
Tune your voice to spread the fame
Of the great Jehovah's name.

4 All who dwell beneath his light,
In his praise your hearts unite;
While the stream of song is pour'd,
Praise and magnify the Lord.

PSALM 116.—7's.

1 This shall be the peoples' cry,
Praise the Lord, the Lord most high ;
Heav'n and earth, on you we call,
Praise the Lord—the Lord of all.

2 Praise Him, all ye hosts above,
In the Paradise of love ;
Sun and moon, your voices raise ;
Sing, ye stars, your Maker's praise.

3 Earth, from all thy depths below,
Ocean's hallelujahs flow :
Lightning, vapor, wind, and storm,
Hail and snow, His word perform.

4 Hills and mountains, burst in song,
Rivers, roll in praise along ;
Clap your hands, ye trees, and hail
God, who comes in every gale.

5 Birds, on wings of rapture soar,
Warble round His temple door ;
Sounds of joy from herds and flocks,
Echo back, ye vales and rocks.

6 Let His truth by babes be told,
And His wonders by the old ;
Youths and maidens, with delight,
Here in hymns of praise unite.

7 High above all height His throne,
Excellent His name alone ;
Every being, bless that name,
All His works, His pow'r proclaim.

PART II.—HYMNS.

ADORATION AND PRAISE FOR CREATION, PROVIDENCE, AND REDEMPTION.

HYMN 1.—L. M.

1 Come, O my soul, in sacred lays
   Attempt the great Creator's praise:
   But, O, what tongue can speak his fame?
   What verse can reach the lofty theme?

2 Enthroned amid the radiant spheres,
   He glory like a garment wears;
   To form a robe of light divine,
   Ten thousand suns around him shine.

3 In all our Maker's grand designs,
   Almighty power, with wisdom, shines;
   His works through all this wondrous frame,
   Declare the glory of his name.

4 Raised on devotion's lofty wing,
   Do thou, my soul, his glories sing;
   And let his praise employ thy tongue
   Till listening worlds shall join the song.

FOR CREATION.

HYMN 2.—L. M.

1 Eternal Power! whose high abode
Becomes the grandeur of a God:
Infinite lengths beyond the bounds
Where stars revolve their little rounds.

2 Thee, while the first archangel sings,
He hides his face behind his wings;
And ranks of shining thrones around
Fall worshipping, and spread the ground.

3 Lord, what shall earth and ashes do?
We would adore our Maker too:
From sin and dust to thee we cry,
The Great, the Holy, and the High.

4 Earth from afar hath heard thy fame,
And worms have learnt to lisp thy name:
But oh! the glories of thy mind
Leave all our soaring thoughts behind.

5 God is in heaven, and men below;
Be short our tunes: our words be few:
A solemn rev'rence checks our songs,
And praise sits silent on our tongues.

HYMN 3.—C. M.

1 Eternal Wisdom, thee we praise;
Thee all thy creatures sing;
While with thy name, rocks, hills, and seas,
And heaven's high palace, ring.

2 Thy hand, how wide it spread the sky;
How glorious to behold!
Tinged with a blue of heavenly dye,
And decked with sparkling gold.

3 Thy glories blaze all nature round,
    And strike the gazing sight,
  Through skies, and seas, and solid ground,
    With terror and delight.

4 Almighty power, and equal skill,
    Shine through the worlds abroad,
  Our souls with vast amazement fill,
    And speak the builder, God.

5 But still, the wonders of thy grace
    Our warmer passions move;
  Here we behold our Saviour's face,
    And here adore his love.

HYMN 4.—C. M.

1 The Lord our God is clothed with might;
    The winds obey his will;
  He speaks, and in the heavenly height
    The rolling sun stands still.

2 Rebel, ye waves, and o'er the land
    With threatening aspect roar;
  The Lord uplifts his awful hand,
    And chains you to the shore.

3 Ye winds of night, your force combine;
    Without his high behest,
  Ye shall not, in the mountain-pine,
    Disturb the sparrow's nest.

4 His voice sublime is heard afar;
    In distant peals it dies;
  He binds the whirlwinds to his car,
    And sweeps the howling skies.

5 Ye nations bend; in rev'rence bend;
   Ye monarchs, wait his nod,
And bid the choral song ascend
   To celebrate our God.

HYMN 5.—L. M.

1 Look up, ye saints, direct your eyes
To him who dwells above the skies;
With your glad notes his praise rehearse,
Who form'd the mighty universe.

2 He spake, and from the womb of night,
At once sprang up the cheering light;
Him, discord heard, and at his nod
Beauty awoke, and spoke the God.

3 The word he gave, th' obedient sun
Began his glorious race to run;
Nor silver moon, nor stars delay,
To glide along th' ethereal way.

4 Teeming with life, air, earth, and sea,
Obey th' Almighty's high decree;
To every tribe he gives their food,
Then speaks the whole divinely good.

5 But, to complete the woundrous plan,
From earth and dust he fashions man;
In man the last, in him the best,
The Master's image stands confest.

6 Lord, while thy glorious works I view,
Form thou my heart and life anew;
Here, bid thy purest light to shine,
And beauty glow with charms divine.

HYMN 6.—10's & 11's.

1 O worship the King, all glorious above,
And gratefully sing his wonderful love,
Our Shield and Defender, the Ancient of Days,
Pavilioned in splendor, and girded with praise.

2 O, tell of his might, and sing of his grace,
Whose robe is the light, whose canopy, space;
His chariots of wrath the deep thunder-clouds form,
And dark is his path on the wings of the storm.

3 Thy bountiful care what tongue can recite!
It breathes in the air, it shines in the light,
It streams from the hills, it descends to the plain,
And sweetly distils in the dew and the rain.

4 Frail children of dust, and feeble as frail,
In thee do we trust, nor find thee to fail;
Thy mercies how tender! how firm to the end!
Our Maker, Defender, Preserver, and Friend.

5 Father Almighty, how faithful thy love!
While angels delight to hymn thee above,
The humbler creation, though feeble their lays,
With true adoration shall lisp to thy praise.

HYMN 7.—8's & 7's.

1 God of all created wonder;
God of countless orbs of light;
God of rain, and wind and thunder,
God of morning, noon, and night;
Blessed be thy name forever,
Blessed be thy glorious reign;
Thy great system faileth never,
All thy works in truth remain.

2 God of valley, plain, and mountain,
God of garden, field, and wood;

FOR CREATION. 89

God of river, stream, and fountain,
  God of all created good;
Thy great system faileth never,
  All thy works in truth remain:
Blessed be thy name forever;
  Blessed be thy glorious reign.

3 God of mercy, God of heaven,
  God of faith, and hope, and love,
Thankful are we that 'tis given
  Us to raise our hopes above.
Gracious Father! by thy Spirit
  In thy word may we be led
Safely, till we shall inherit
  All that thou hast promised.

HYMN 8.—L. P. M.

1 Let all on earth their voices raise,
  To sing a lofty psalm of praise,
    And bless the great Jehovah's name;
  His glory let the heathen know,
  His wonders to the nations show,
    And all his works of grace proclaim.

2 He framed the globe, he spread the sky,
  And all the shining worlds on high;
    He reigns complete in glory there:
  His beams are majesty and light,
  His glories, how divinely bright!
    His temple, how divinely fair!

3 Let heaven be glad, let earth rejoice,
  Let ocean lift its roaring voice,
    Proclaming loud, "Jehovah reigns!"

For joy let fertile valleys sing,
And tuneful groves their tribute bring
  To Him whose power the world sustains.

4 Come the great day, the glorious hour,
When earth shall own his sovereign power,
  And barbarous nations fear his name;
Then shall the universe confess
The beauty of his holiness,
  And in his courts his grace proclaim.

HYMN 9.—S. M.

1   O Lord, our heavenly king,
    Thy name is all divine;
Thy glories round the earth are spread,
    And o'er the heavens they shine.

2   When to thy works on high,
    I raise my wondering eyes,
And see the moon, complete in light,
    Adorn the darksome skies.

3   When I survey the stars,
    And all their shining forms,
Lord, what is man—that worthless thing,
    Akin to dust and worms?

4   Lord, what is worthless man,
    That thou shouldst love him so?
Next to thine angels is he placed,
    And lord of all below.

5   How rich thy bounties are!
    How wondrous are thy ways!

That from the dust, thy power should frame
  A monument of praise.
Let praise to God arise,
  To God, the sovereign king;
For love so boundless and divine,
  Thy praises, Lord, we sing.

HYMN 10.—8's & 7's.

1 Bright the vision that delighted
    Once the sight of Judah's seer;
  Sweet the countless tongues united
    To entrance the prophet's ear,
  Round the Lord in glory seated,
    Cherubim and seraphim
  Filled his temple, and repeated
    Each to each th' alternate hymn:—

2 "Lord, thy glory fills the heaven;
    Earth is with its fulness stored;
  Unto thee be glory given,
    Holy, holy, holy, Lord!"
  Heaven is still with glory ringing;
    Earth takes up the angels' cry,
  "Holy, holy, holy," singing,
    "Lord of hosts, the Lord most high!"

3 Ever thus in God's high praises,
    Brethren, let our tongues unite,
  Whilst our thoughts his greatness raises,
    And our love his gifts excite.
  With his seraph train before him,
    With his holy church below,
  Thus conspire we to adore him,
    Bid we thus our anthem flow:—

4 "Lord, thy glory fills the heaven;
    Earth is with its fulness stored;
Unto thee be glory given,
    Holy, holy, holy Lord!"
Thus thy glorious name confessing,
    We adopt thy angels' cry,
"Holy, holy, holy," blessing
    Thee, the Lord of hosts most high!

HYMN 11.—L. M.

1 JEHOVAH reigns, his throne is high,
His robes are light and majesty;
His glory shines with beams so bright,
No mortal can sustain the sight.

2 His terrors keep the world in awe,
His justice guards his holy law,
His love reveals a smiling face,
His truth and promise seal the grace.

3 Through all his works what wisdom shines?
He baffles Satan's deep designs;
His power is sovereign to fulfil
The noblest counsels of his will.

4 Thus glorious, will he condescend
To be my Father and my Friend?
Then let my songs with angels join;
Heaven is secure, if God is mine.

HYMN 12.—8's & 7's.

1 PRAISE the Lord! ye heav'ns adore him;
    Praise him, angels, in the height;
Sun and moon rejoice before him,
    Praise him all ye stars and light.

2 Praise the Lord! for he hath spoken,
    Worlds his mighty voice obey'd;
  Laws which never shall be broken,
    For their guidance hath he made.

3 Praise the Lord! for he is glorious,
    Never shall his promise fail;
  God will make his saints victorious,
    Sin and death shall not prevail.

4 Praise the God of our salvation!
    Hosts on high his pow'r proclaim;
  Heav'n and earth, and all creation,
    Laud and magnify his name.

HYMN 13.—8's.

1 Thou art, O God, the life and light
    Of all this wondrous world we see:
  Its glow by day, its smiles by night,
    Are but reflections caught from thee:
  Where'er we turn, thy glories shine,
  And all things fair and bright are thine.

2 When day with farewell beam delays
    Among the opening clouds of even,
  And we can almost think we gaze
    Through opening vistas into heaven,
  Those hues that mark the sun's decline,
  So soft, so radiant, Lord, are thine.

3 When night with wings of starry gloom
    O'ershadows all the earth and skies,
  Like some dark beauteous bird, whose plume
    Is sparkling with a thousand dyes,
  That sacred gloom, those fires divine,
  So grand, so countless, Lord, are thine.

4 When youthful spring around us breathes,
   Thy Spirit warms her fragrant sigh,
And every flower that summer wreathes
   Is born beneath that kindling eye:
Where'er we turn thy glories shine,
And all things fair and bright are thine.

HYMN 14.—L. M.

1 All-powerful, self-existent God,
   Who all creation dost sustain!
Thou wast, and art, and art to come,
   And everlasting is thy reign.

2 Fixed and eternal as thy days,
   Each glorious attribute divine,
Through ages infinite, shall still
   With undiminish'd lustre shine.

3 Fountain of being! Source of good!
   Immutable dost thou remain;
Nor can the shadow of a change
   Obscure the glories of thy reign.

4 Earth may with all her powers dissolve,
   If such the great Creator's will:
But thou forever art the same;
   "I AM" is thy memorial still.

HYMN 15.—C. M.

1 Great God, how infinite art thou!
   How frail and weak are we!
Let the whole race of creatures bow,
   And pay their praise to thee.

FOR CREATION.

2 Thy throne eternal ages stood,
    Ere seas or stars were made:
Thou art the ever-living God,
    Were all the nations dead.

3 Eternity, with all its years,
    Stands present in thy view;
To thee there's nothing old appears;
    Great God! there's nothing new.

4 Our lives through varying scenes are drawn,
    And vex'd with trifling cares,
While thine eternal thought moves on
    Thine undisturbed affairs.

5 Great God! how infinite art thou!
    How frail and weak are we!
Let the whole race of creatures bow,
    And pay their praise to thee.

HYMN 16.—L. M.

1 JEHOVAH reigns, he dwells in light,
Girded with majesty and might;
The world, created by his hands,
Still on its first foundation stands.

2 But ere this spacious world was made,
Or had its first foundation laid,
Thy throne eternal ages stood,
Thyself the ever-living God.

3 Like floods the angry nations rise,
And aim their rage against the skies;
Vain floods, that aim their rage so high!
At thy rebuke the billows die.

4 For ever shall thy throne endure,
   Thy promise stands for ever sure;
   And everlasting holiness
   Becomes the dwellings of thy grace.

HYMN 17.—L. M.

1 Great God! in vain man's narrow view
  Attempts to look thy nature through;
  Our laboring powers with reverence own
  Thy glories never can be known.

2 Not the high seraph's mighty thought,
  Who countless years his God has sought,
  Such wondrous height or depth can find,
  Or fully trace thy boundless mind.

3 Yet, Lord, thy kindness deigns to show
  Enough for mortal minds to know;
  While wisdom, goodness, power divine,
  Though all thy works and conduct shine.

4 Oh, may our souls with rapture trace
  Thy works of nature and of grace!
  Explore thy sacred name, and still
  Press on to know and do thy will!

HYMN 18.—L. M.

1 Praise ye the Lord! 'tis good to raise
  Your hearts and voices in his praise:
  His nature and his works invite
  To make this duty our delight.

2 He form'd the stars, those heavenly flames;
  He counts their numbers, calls their names;
  His wisdom's vast, and knows no bound,—
  A deep where all our thoughts are drown'd.

3 Sing to the Lord! exalt him high,
Who spread the clouds along the sky;
There he prepares the fruitful rain,
Nor lets the drops descend in vain.

4 He makes the grass the hills adorn;
He clothes the smiling fields with corn;
The beasts with food his hands supply,
And the young ravens when they cry.

5 What is the creature's skill or force?
The sprightly man, or warlike horse?
The piercing wit, the active limb?
All these are mean delights for him.

6 But saints are lovely in his sight;
He views his children with delight:
He sees their hope, he knows their fear,
He looks, and loves his image there.

HYMN 19.—L. M. 6 l.

1 Above—below—where'er I gaze,
  Thy guiding finger, Lord, I view,
Traced in the midnight planets' blaze,
  Or glistening in the morning dew;
Whate'er is beautiful or fair,
Is but thine own reflection there.

2 I hear thee in the stormy wind,
  That turns the ocean-wave to foam;
Nor less wondrous power I find,
  When summer airs around me roam:
The tempest and the calm declare
Thyself,—for thou art every where.

3 I find thee in the noon of night,
    And read thy name in every star,
That drinks its splendor from the light,
    That flows from mercy's beaming car:
Thy footstool, Lord, each starry gem
Composes—not thy diadem.

4 And when the radiant orb of light
    Hath tipp'd the mountain-tops with gold,
Smote with the blaze my weary sight
    Shrinks from the wonders I behold:
That ray of glory bright and fair,
Is but thy living shadow there.

5 Thine is the silent noon of night,
    The twilight eve—the dewy morn;
Whate'er is beautiful and bright,
    Thine hands have fashioned to adorn;
Thy glory walks in every sphere,
And all things whisper, " God is here !"

HYMN 20.—C. M.

1 BEGIN the high, celestial strain,
    My raptured soul, and sing
A sacred hymn of grateful praise
    To heaven's almighty King.

2 Ye curling fountains, as ye roll
    Your silver waves along,
Repeat to all your verdant shores
    The subject of the song.

3 Bear it, ye breezes, on your wings,
    To distant climes away,

And round the wide-extended world
　The lofty theme convey.

4 Take up the burden of his name,
　Ye clouds, as ye arise,
To deck with gold the opening morn,
　Or shade the evening skies.

5 Long let it warble round the spheres
　And echo through the sky;
Let angels, with immortal skill,
　Improve the harmony;

6 While we, with sacred rapture fired,
　The blest Creator sing,
And chant our consecrated lays
　To heaven's eternal King.

HYMN 21.—L. M.

1 Awake, my tongue; thy tribute bring
To Him who gave thee power to sing;
Praise Him who is all praise above,
The source of wisdom and of love.

2 How vast his knowledge! how profound!
A depth where all our thoughts are drown'd!
The stars he numbers, and their names
He gives to all those heavenly flames.

3 Through each bright orb above, behold
Ten thousand thousand charms unfold;
Earth, air, and mighty seas combine
To speak his wisdom all divine.

4 But in redemption, O, what grace!
Its wonders, O, what thought can trace!
Here wisdom shines for ever bright;
Praise him, my soul, with sweet delight.

HYMN 22.—C. P. M.

1 Begin, my soul, th' exalted lay,
Let each enraptured thought obey,
   And praise th' Almighty's name:
Lo! heaven and earth, and seas and skies
In one melodious concert rise,
   To swell th' inspiring theme.

2 Thou heaven of heavens, his vast abode,
Ye clouds, proclaim your Maker, God;
   Ye thunders, speak his power.
Lo! on the lightning's fiery wing,
In triumph walks th' eternal King;
   Th' astonished worlds adore.

3 Ye deeps, with roaring billows rise,
To join the thunders of the skies;
   Praise him who bids you roll.
His praise in softer notes declare,
Each whisp'ring breeze of yielding air,
   And breathe it to the soul.

4 Wake, all ye soaring throngs, and sing;
Ye feathered warblers of the spring,
   Harmonious anthems raise
To Him, who shaped your finer mould,
Who tipp'd your glitt'ring wings with gold,
   And tuned your voice to praise.

5 Let man, by nobler passions sway'd,
Let man, in God's own image made,
   His breath in praise employ;
Spread wide his Maker's name around,
Till heaven shall echo back the sound
   In songs of holy joy.

FOR CREATION.

HYMN 23.—C. M.

1 Lord of the world's majestic frame!
 Stupendous are thy ways;
Thy various works declare thy name,
 And all resound thy praise.

2 Those mighty orbs proclaim thy power,
 Whose motions speak thy skill;
And, on the wings of every hour,
 We read thy glory still.

3 And while these radiant globes of light,
 That shine from pole to pole,
In silent harmony unite,
 To praise thee as they roll;

4 O, shall not we of human race
 The glorious concert join?
Shall not the children of thy grace
 Attempt the theme divine?

5 Yes, this shall be our best employ
 Through life's uncertain days;
Till in the realms of boundless joy
 We join in loftier praise.

HYMN 24.—7's.

1 Thou, who art enthroned above,
Thou, by whom we live and move,
O, how sweet, with joyful tongue,
To resound thy praise in song!
When the morning paints the skies,
When the sparkling stars arise,
All thy favors to rehearse,
And give thanks in grateful verse!

2 Sweet the day of sacred rest,
   When devotion fills the breast;
   When we dwell within thy house,
   Hear thy word and pay our vows,
   Notes to heaven's high mansions raise,
   Fill its courts with joyful praise;
   With repeated hymns proclaim
   Great Jehovah's awful name!

3 From thy works our joys arise,
   O, thou only good and wise!
   Who thy wonders can declare?
   How profound thy counsels are!
   Warm our hearts with sacred fire;
   Grateful fervors still inspire;
   All our powers, with all their might,
   Ever in thy praise unite.

HYMN 25.—C. M.

1 I sing th' almighty power of God,
   That made the mountains rise,
   That spread the flowing seas abroad,
   And built the lofty skies.

2 I sing the wisdom that ordain'd
   The sun to rule the day;
   The moon, that shines at his command,
   While all the stars obey.

3 I sing the goodness of the Lord,
   That fill'd the earth with food;
   He form'd the creatures by his word,
   And then pronounced them good.

4 There's not a plant or flower below
    But makes thy glories known ;
And clouds arise, and tempests blow,
    By orders from thy throne.

5 Creatures that borrow life from thee
    Are subject to thy care ;
There's not a place where we can flee
    But God is present there.

6 His hand is my perpetual guard:
    He keeps me with his eye:
Why should I then forget the Lord,
    Who is for ever nigh ?

HYMN 26.—C. M.

1 O THOU, my light, my life, my joy,
    My glory, and my all;
Unsent by thee, no good can come,
    No evil can befall.

2 Such are thy schemes of providence,
    And methods of thy grace,
That I may safely trust in thee
    Through all the wilderness.

3 'T is thine outstretch'd and powerful arm
    Upholds me in the way;
And thy rich bounty well supplies
    The wants of every day.

4 For such compassions, O my God!
    Ten thousand thanks are due;
For such compassions, I esteem
    Ten thousand thanks too few.

HYMN 27.—C. M.

1 God, in the high and holy place,
    Looks down upon the spheres;
Yet, in his providence and grace,
    To every eye appears.

2 He bows the heavens! the mountains stand
    A highway for our God:
He walks amid the desert land;
    'Tis Eden where he trod.

3 In every stream his bounty flows,
    Diffusing joy and wealth;
In every breeze his spirit blows,
    The breath of life and health.

4 His blessings fall in plenteous showers
    Upon the lap of earth,
That teems with foliage, fruits, and flowers,
    And rings with infant mirth.

5 If God hath made this world so fair,
    Where sin and death abound,
How beautiful, beyond compare,
    Will paradise be found!

HYMN 28.—8's & 7's.

1 Praise to thee, thou great Creator!
    Praise to thee from every tongue!
Join my soul, with every creature,
    Join the universal song.

2 For ten thousand blessings given,
    For the hope of future joy,
Sound his praise through earth and heaven,
    Sound Jehovah's praise on high!

HYMN 29.—s. m.

1 Great God! at thy command
　Seasons in order rise;
Thy power and love in concert reign
　Through earth, and seas, and skies.

2 How balmy is the air!
　How warm the solar beams!
And, to refresh the ground, the rains
　Descend in gentle streams.

3 With grateful praise we own
　Thy providential hand,
While grass for kine, and herbs and corn
　For men, enrich the land.

4 But greater still the gift
　Of thine incarnate Son:
By him forgiveness, peace, and joy,
　Through endless ages run.

HYMN 30.—s. m.

1 The Lord my Shepherd is,
　I shall be well supplied:
Since he is mine and I am his,
　What can I want beside?

2 He leads me to the place
　Where heavenly pasture grows,
Where living waters gently pass,
　And full salvation flows.

3 If e'er I go astray,
　He doth my soul reclaim,
And guides me in his own right way,
　For his most holy name.

4 While he affords his aid,
   I cannot yield to fear;
Though I should walk through death's dark [shade,
   My Shepherd's with me there.

5 In sight of all my foes
   Thou dost my table spread,
My cup with blessings overflows,
   And joy exalts my head.

6 The bounties of thy love
   Shall crown my foll'wing days;
Nor from thy house will I remove,
   Nor cease to speak thy praise.

HYMN 31.—C. M.

1 O God, on thee we all depend,
   On thy paternal care;
Thou wilt the Father and the Friend
   In every act appear.

2 With open hand and lib'ral heart
   Thou wilt our wants supply;
The needful blessings still impart,
   And no good thing deny.

3 Our Father knows what's good and fit,
   And wisdom guides his love;
To thine appointments we submit,
   And every choice approve.

4 In thy paternal love and care,
   With cheerful hearts we trust;
Thy tender mercies boundless are,
   And all thy thoughts are just.

5 We cannot want while God provides;
  What he ordains is best;
  And heaven, whate'er we want besides,
  Will give eternal rest.

HYMN 32.—L. M.

1 My helper, God! I bless his name,
  The same his power, his grace the same;
  The tokens of his friendly care
  Open and crown, and close the year.

2 I 'midst ten thousand dangers stand,
  Supported by his guardian hand;
  And see, when I survey my ways,
  Ten thousand monuments of praise.

3 Thus far his arm hath led me on;
  Thus far I make his mercy known;
  And while I tread this desert land,
  New mercies shall new songs demand.

HYMN 33.—C. M.

1 Father, 't is thine each day to yield,
    Our wants a fresh supply;
  To clothe the lilies of the field,
    And hear the ravens cry.

2 Thy love in all thy works we see,
    Thy promise, Lord, we plead,
  And humbly cast our care on thee,
    Who knowest all our need.

3 Let not the world engage our love,
    Nor care our bosom fill;
  But fix our hearts on things above,
    That we may do thy will.

4 The comfort of thy light bestow;
    Our faith, O Lord, increase,
And grant thy presence here below,
    The dawn of endless peace.

HYMN 34.—L. M.

1 Great God, we sing that mighty hand,
By which supported still we stand;
The opening year thy mercy shows;
That mercy crowns it till it close.

2 By day, by night, at home, abroad,
Still are we guarded by our God;
By his incessant bounty fed,
By his unerring counsel led.

3 With grateful hearts the past we own;
The future, all to us unknown,
We to thy guardian care commit,
And peaceful leave before thy feet.

4 In scenes exalted or depress'd,
Thou art our joy, and thou our rest;
Thy goodness all our hopes shall raise,
Adored through all our changing days.

HYMN 35.—L. M.

1 Eternal Source of every joy,
Thy praise may well our lips employ,
While in thy temple we appear,
Whose goodness crowns the circling year.

2 Wide as the wheels of nature roll,
Thy hand supports the steady pole;
The sun is taught by thee to rise,
And darkness when to veil the skies.

3 The flow'ry spring, at thy command,
Embalms the air, and paints the land;
The summer rays with vigor shine,
To raise the corn, and cheer the vine.

4 Thy hand in autumn richly pours
Though all our coasts abundant stores;
And winters, soften'd by thy care,
No more a dreary aspect wear.

5 Still be the cheerful homage paid
With morning light and evening shade;
Seasons, and months, and weeks, and days,
Demand successive songs of praise.

HYMN 36.—L. M.

1 God of the rolling year, to thee
   Our songs shall rise, whose bounty pours
In many a goodly gift, with free
   And lib'ral hand, our autumn stores;
No firstlings of our flock we slay,
   No soaring clouds of incense rise,
But on thy hallow'd shrine we lay
   Our grateful hearts in sacrifice.

2 Borne on thy breath, the lap of spring
   Was heaped with many a blooming flower;
And smiling summer joyed to bring
   The sunshine and the gentle shower;
And autumn's rich luxuriance now,
   The rip'ning seed, the bursting shell,
The golden sheaf, and laden bough,
   The fulness of thy bounty tell.

3 And here shall rise our song to thee,
   Where lengthen'd vales and pastures lie,

And streams go singing, wild and free,
    Beneath a blue and smiling sky;
Where ne'er was rear'd a mortal throne,
    Where crown'd oppressors never trod;
Here, at the throne of heaven alone,
    Shall man in rev'rence bow to God.

HYMN 37.—7's.

1 Praise to God, immortal praise,
For the love that crowns our days:
Bounteous Source of every joy,
Let thy praise our tongues employ:
All to thee, our God, we owe,
Source whence all our blessings flow.

2 All the blessings of the fields,
All the stores the garden yields,
Flocks that whiten all the plain,
Yellow sheaves of ripen'd grain:
Lord, for these our souls shall raise
Grateful vows and solemn praise.

3 Clouds that drop their fatt'ning dews,
Suns that genial warmth diffuse,
All the plenty summer pours,
Autumn's rich o'erflowing stores;
Lord, for these our souls shall raise
Grateful vows and solemn praise.

4 Peace, prosperity, and health,
Private bliss and public wealth,
Knowledge, with its gladd'ning streams,
Pure religion's holier beams:
Lord, for these our souls shall raise
Grateful vows and solemn praise.

FOR PROVIDENTIAL FAVORS.

HYMN 38—s. m.

1 The flowers about our path,
    The sun that shines above,
  And every thing around, beneath,
    Proclaim Thee, God of love.

2 Yes, all things tell of Thee—
    The meadows and the trees,
  The ever-bounding, restless sea,
    The shower and the breeze.

3 And, Oh! shall we not raise
    A glad triumphant strain?
  If meaner creatures hymn thy praise,
    Sure we cannot refrain.

4 We for whom thou hast giv'n
    Thine own most blessed Son,
  To make us chosen heirs of heaven,
    To raise us to a throne.

5 He suffered and he died
    That we in him might live;
  His crown of thorns and pierced side
    Our crowns of glory give.

6 Then to our God and King
    Our noblest praise be given;
  And we will trust, e'er long, to sing
    A worthier strain in heaven.

HYMN 39.—p. m.

1 From the recess of a lowly spirit,
  My humble prayer ascends: O Father, hear it,
  Upsoaring on the wings of fear and meekness,
        Forgive its weakness.

2 I know, I feel, how mean, how unworthy
The trembling sacrifice I pour before thee,
What can I offer in thy presence holy,
    But sin and folly.

3 For in thy sight, who every bosom viewest,
Cold are our warmest vows, and vain our truest;
Thoughts of a hurrying hour, our lips repeat them,
    Our hearts forget them.

4 We see thy hand, it leads us, it supports us,
We hear thy voice, it counsels and it courts us,
And then we turn away—and still thy kindness
    Pardons our blindness.

5 And still thy rain descends, thy sun is glowing,
Fruits ripen round, flowers are beneath us blowing,
And, as if man were some deserving creature,
    Joys cover nature.

6 O, how long-suffering, Lord! but thou delightest
To win with love the wand'ring,—thou invitest,
By smiles of mercy, not by frowns or terrors,
    Man from his errors.

7 Who can resist thy gentle call, appealing
To every gen'rous thought, and grateful feeling,
That voice paternal, whisp'ring, watching ever?
    My bosom never.

8 Father and Savior! plant within this bosom
These seeds of holiness, and bid them blossom
In fragrance and in beauty, bright and vernal,
    And spring eternal.

HYMN 40.—L. M.

1 Praise for the book of saving truth,
  To guilty man so freely giv'n;
Praise for this guide of age and youth,
  Directing to our promised heaven.

2 All hail the grace ! this gift of God
    Unfolds a scheme of matchless love—
  Reveals the path which Jesus trod—
    Withdraws the veil from things above.

3 Free as the light, it beams afar,
    And breathes sweet hope where mis'ry dwells;
  In darkest hours, this quenchless star,
    A brighter, happier day foretells.

4 Midst dungeon walls of endless gloom,
    On torturing rack, or fiercest fire ;
  If rich or poor, in age or bloom,
    This shall a martyr's faith inspire.

5 Thence living waters constant rise,
    To cheer the faint and burden'd mind;
  Food which immortal life supplies
    To every tribe of human kind.

6 My Bible ! more than gold to me—
    My guide in youth, a staff for age ;
  The Savior's love revealed in thee
    Shall cheer me through life's pilgrimage.

HYMN 41.—C. M.

1 FATHER of mercies, in thy word
    What endless glory shines !
  Forever be thy name adored
    For these celestial lines.

2 'T is here the tree of knowledge grows,
    And yields a free repast;
  Here purer sweets than nature knows
    Invite the longing taste.

3 'T is here the Savior's welcome voice
   Spreads heavenly peace around;
And life, and everlasting joys
   Attend the blissful sound.

4 O, may these heavenly pages be
   My ever dear delight;
And still new beauties may I see,
   And still increasing light!

5 Divine Instructor, gracious Lord,
   Be thou forever near;
Teach me to love thy sacred word,
   And view my Savior here.

HYNM 42.—L. M.

1 The heavens declare thy glory, Lord;
   In every star thy wisdom shines;
But when our eyes behold thy word,
   We read thy name in fairer lines.

2 The rolling sun, the changing light,
   And nights and days, thy power confess;
But the blest volume thou hast writ,
   Reveals thy justice and thy grace.

3 Sun, moon, and stars convey thy praise
   Round the whole earth, and never stand;
So when thy truth began its race,
   It touched and glanced on every land.

4 Nor shall thy glorious gospel rest,
   Till through the world thy truth has run:
Till Christ has all the nations bless'd,
   That see the light or feel the sun.

5 Great Sun of righteousness! arise,
   Bless the dark world with heavenly light;
 Thy gospel makes the simple wise,
   Thy laws are pure, thy judgments right.

6 Thy noblest wonders here we view,
   In souls renewed, and sins forgiven:
 Lord, cleanse from sin, our souls renew,
   And let thy word guide us to heaven.

HYMN 43.—L. M.

1 Thy word, O Lord! is light and food,
 The law of truth, and source of good:
 There thou hast pointed out my way
 To pardon and perpetual day.

2 May I receive it, Lord, as thine,
 Receive it as the word divine,
 With firm assent, with listening ear,
 With bending heart, and filial fear.

3 Make me to know its saving might,
 Its quickening power, its cheering light;
 May it my stubborn heart subdue,
 And still my sinful soul renew.

4 O let it richly dwell within,
 To keep me from the snares of sin,
 And guide me still to choose my way,
 That I no more may go astray.

5 Thus shall I stand approved of God,
 And follow still the heavenly road;
 Here, like an heir of heaven shall live,
 And there, a crown of life receive.

HYMN 44.—C. M.

1 With my whole heart I've sought thy face,
  Oh let me never stray
From thy commands, O God of grace,
  Nor tread the sinner's way.

2 Thy word I've hid within my heart
  To keep my conscience clean,
And be an everlasting guard
  From every rising sin.

3 I'm a companion of the saints,
  Who fear and love the Lord;
My sorrows rise, my nature faints,
  When men transgress thy word.

4 While sinners do thy gospel wrong,
  My spirit stands in awe;
My soul abhors a lying tongue,
  But loves thy righteous law.

5 My heart with sacred rev'rence hears
  The threat'nings of thy word;
My flesh with holy trembling fears
  The judgments of the Lord.

6 My God, I long, I hope, I wait
  For thy salvation still;
Thy holy law is my delight,
  And I obey thy will.

HYMN 45.—C. M.

1 Great God, with wonder and with praise
  On all thy works I look;
But still thy wisdom, power, and grace
  Shine brightest in thy book.

FOR THE SCRIPTURES. 117

2 Here are my choicest treasures hid;
   Here my best comfort lies;
Here my desires are satisfied;
   And here my hopes arise.

3 Lord, make me understand thy law;
   Show what my faults have been;
And from thy gospel let me draw
   The pardon of my sin.

HYMN 46.—L. M.

1 How precious is thy word, O God!
   'T is for our light and guidance given;
It sheds a lustre all abroad,
   And points the path to bliss and heaven.

2 It fills the soul with sweet delight;
   And quickens its inactive powers;
It sets our wand'ring footsteps right,
   Displays thy love and kindles ours.

3 Its promises rejoice our hearts;
   Its doctrines are divinely true;
Knowledge and pleasure it imparts;
   It comforts and instructs us too.

4 Ye favored lands, who have this word!
   Ye saints, who feel its saving power!
Unite your tongues to praise the Lord,
   And his distinguish'd grace adore.

HYMN 47.—L. M.

1 With all my powers of heart and tongue,
   I'll praise my Maker in my song;
Angels shall hear the notes I raise,
   Approve the song, and join the praise.

PRAISE TO GOD

2 To God I cried, when troubles rose,
  He heard me, and subdued my foes;
  He did my rising fears control,
  And strength diffused through all my soul.

3 Amid a thousand snares I stand,
  Upheld and guarded by thy hand;
  Thy words my fainting soul revive,
  And keep my dying faith alive.

4 I'll sing thy truth and mercy, Lord;
  I'll sing the wonders of thy word;
  Not all thy works and names below
  So much thy power and glory show.

HYMN 48.—l. m.

1 'Twas by an order from the Lord,
  The ancient prophets spoke his word;
  His Spirit did their tongues inspire,
  And warm their hearts with heavenly fire.

2 Great God, mine eyes with pleasure look
  On all the pages of thy book;
  There my Redeemer's face I see,
  And read his name who died for me.

3 Let the false raptures of the mind
  Be lost and vanish in the wind;
  Here I can fix my hope secure;
  This is thy word, and must endure.

HYMN 49.—l. m.

1 I love the volume of thy word;
  What light and joy those leaves afford
    To souls benighted and distrest!

Thy precepts guide my doubtful way;
Thy fear forbids my feet to stray;
  Thy promise leads my heart to rest.

2 Thy threat'nings wake my slumb'ring eyes,
  And warn me where my danger lies;
    But 't is thy blessed gospel, Lord,
That makes my guilty conscience clean,
Converts my soul, subdues my sin,
    And gives a free, but large reward.

3 Who knows the error of his thoughts?
My God forgive my secret faults,
  And from presumptuous sins restrain;
Accept my poor attempts of praise,
That I have read thy book of grace,
  And book of nature, not in vain.

HYMN 50.—L. M.

1 God, in the gospel of his Son,
Makes his eternal counsels known;
'T is here his richest mercy shines,
And truth is drawn in fairest lines.

2 Here Jesus, in ten thousand ways,
His soul-attracting charms displays,
Recounts his poverty and pains,
And tells his love in melting strains.

3 Wisdom its dictates here imparts,
To form our minds, to cheer our hearts;
Its influence makes the sinner live;
It bids the drooping saint revive.

4 Our raging passions it controls,
And comfort yields to contrite souls;

It brings a better world in view,
And guides us all our journey through.

5 May this blest volume ever lie
Close to my heart, and near my eye,
Till life's last hour my soul engage,
And be my chosen heritage.

HYMN 51.—C. M.

1 What glory gilds the sacred page!
  Majestic, like the sun,
It gives a light to every age;
  It gives, but borrows none.

2 The hand that gave it still supplies
  The gracious light and heat;
His truths upon the nations rise;
  They rise but never set.

3 Let everlasting thanks be thine
  For such a bright display,
As makes a world of darkness shine
  With beams of heavenly day.

HYMN 52.—8's & 7's.

1 Praise to Him, by whose kind favor,
  Heavenly truth has reached our ears!
May its sweet reviving savor,
  Fill our hearts and calm our fears.

2 Truth! how sacred is the treasure!
  Teach us, Lord, its worth to know;
Vain the hope, and short the pleasure,
  Which from other sources flow.

3 What of truth we have been hearing,
  Fix, O Lord, in every heart;
In the day of Christ's appearing
  May we share thy people's part.

HYMN 53.—C. M.

1 Let all the heathen writers join
    To form one perfect book;
  Great God, if once compared with thine,
    How mean their writings look!

2 Not the most perfect rules they gave
    Could show one sin forgiven,
  Nor lead a step beyond the grave;
    But thine conduct to heaven.

3 I've seen an end of what we call
    Perfection here below;
  How short the pow'rs of nature fall,
    And can no further go.

4 Yet men would fain be just with God,
    By works their hands have wrought;
  But thy commands, exceeding broad,
    Extend to every thought.

HYMN 54.—C. M.

1 Let others boast of wealth or power,
    And glory in their pride:
  Thy word, O God, we value more,
    Than all the world beside.

2 Here mines of knowledge, love, and joy,
    Are open to our sight;

    The purest gold without alloy,
      And gems divinely bright.

3 The counsels of redeeming grace
      These sacred leaves unfold,
    And here the Savior's lovely face
      Our raptur'd eyes behold.

4 Here light descending from above,
      Directs our doubtful feet;
    Here promises of heavenly love
      Our ardent wishes meet.

5 Our num'rous griefs are here redress'd,
      And all our wants supplied;
    Naught we can ask to make us blest
      Is in this book denied.

6 For these inestimable gains,
      That so enrich the mind,
    O may we search with eager pains,
      Assured that we shall find.

HYMN 55.—8's & 7's.

1 WHAT a mercy, what a treasure
      We possess in God's own word,
    Where we read with sacred pleasure,
      Of the love of Christ our Lord.
    That blest word reveals the Savior
      Whom we all so deeply need,
    Oh, what mercy, love, and favor,
      That for sinners Christ should bleed.

2 While each wretched heathen nation
      Nothing knows, dear Lord, of thee;

In this happy land, salvation
　Clearly is revealed to me.
Oh, the blessedness of knowing
　Christ our Savior's precious love;
Freely on us all bestowing
　Grace and mercy from above.

HYMN 56.—C. M.

1 Laden with guilt and full of fears,
　　I fly to thee, my Lord;
　And not a glimpse of hope appears,
　　But in thy written word.

2 The volume of my Father's grace
　　Does all my grief assuage;
　Here I behold my Savior's face
　　In almost ev'ry page.

3 This is the field where hidden lies
　　The pearl of price unknown;
　That merchant is divinely wise,
　　Who makes the pearl his own.

4 Here consecrated water flows,
　　To quench my thirst of sin;
　Here the fair tree of knowledge grows,
　　Nor danger dwells therein.

5 This is the judge which ends the strife,
　　Where wit and reason fail;
　My guide to everlasting life,
　　Through all this gloomy vale.

6 O may thy counsels, mighty God,
　　My roving feet command;
　Nor I forsake the happy road,
　　Which leads to thy right hand.

HYMN 57.—7's.

1 When in silence, o'er the deep,
Darkness kept its death-like sleep;
Soon as God his mandate spoke,
Light in wondrous beauty broke.

2 But a beam of holier light
Gilded Bethlehem's lonely night,
When the glory of the Lord,
Mercy's sunlight, shone abroad.

3 "Peace on earth, good-will to men,"
Burst the glorious anthem then:
Angels, bending from above,
Joined that strain of holy love.

4 Floating o'er the waves of time,
Comes to us that song sublime,
Bearing to the pilgrim's ear,
Words to soothe, sustain, and cheer.

5 For creation's blessed light,
Praise to thee, thou God of might!
Seraph-strains thy name should bless,
For the Sun of Righteousness!

HYMN 58.—C. M.

1 Glory to God, and peace on earth,
Was once by angels sung;
Glad tidings of a Savior's birth
Through plains of Bethlehem rung.

2 He came to make the feeble strong,
To heal the deaf and blind,
To give the dumb the voice of song,
And free the captive mind.

3 He came the light of life to show,
    The true and living way;
Where streams of joy unceasing flow,
    And lead to endless day.

4 Glory to God! our hearts acclaim;
    O, haste the happy time,
When songs shall sound the Savior's name
    O'er every distant clime.

HYMN 59.—L. M.

1 Now to the Lord a noble song!
    Awake, my soul; awake, my tongue;
Hosanna to th' eternal name,
    And all his boundless love proclaim.

2 See where it shines in Jesus' face,
    The brightest image of his grace;
God, in the person of his Son,
    Has all his mightiest works outdone.

3 The spacious earth and spreading flood,
    Proclaim the wise and powerful God;
And thy rich glories from afar
    Sparkle in every rolling star.

4 But in his looks a glory stands,—
    The noblest labor of thine hands;
The pleasing lustre of his eyes,
    Outshines the wonders of the skies.

5 Grace! 't is a sweet, a charming theme;
    My thoughts rejoice at Jesus' name;
Ye angels, dwell upon the sound!
    Ye heavens, reflect it to the ground!

HYMN 60.—C. M.

1 Thy goodness, Lord, our souls confess,
    Thy goodness we adore,
  A spring whose blessings never fail,
    A sea without a shore.

2 Sun, moon, and stars thy love attest,
    In every golden ray:
  Love draws the curtain of the night,
    And love brings back the day.

3 Thy bounty every season crowns,
    With all the bliss it yields;
  With joyful clusters load the vines—
    With strength'ning grain, the fields.

4 But chiefly thy compassion, Lord,
    Is in the gospel seen;
  There like a sun, thy mercy shines,
    Without a cloud between.

5 Pardon, acceptance, peace, and joy,
    Through Jesus' name is given;
  He on the cross was lifted high,
    That we might rise to heaven.

HYMN 61.—C. M.

1 Begin my tongue some heavenly theme,
    And speak some boundless thing,—
  The mighty works, or mightier name
    Of our eternal King.

2 Tell of his wondrous faithfulness,
    And sound his power abroad;

Sing the sweet promise of his grace,
   And the performing God.

3 Proclaim—" Salvation from the Lord,
   For wretched, dying men ;"
His hand has wrote the sacred word,
   With an immortal pen.

4 His word of grace is sure and strong,
   As that which built the skies :
The voice that rolls the stars along
   Spoke all the promises.

HYMN 62.—L. M.

1 Thy favors, Lord, surprise our souls;
   Will th' Eternal dwell with us?
What canst thou find beneath the poles,
   To tempt thy chariot downward thus?

2 Still might he fill his starry throne,
   And please his ears with Gabriel's songs;
But heavenly Majesty comes down,
   And bows to hearken to our tongues.

3 Great God! what poor returns we pay,
   For love so infinite as thine !
Words are but air, and tongues but clay,
   But thy compassion's all divine !

HYMN 63.—L. M.

1 How oft have sin and Satan strove
   To rend my soul from thee, my God !
But everlasting is thy love,
   And Jesus seals it with his blood.

2 The oath and promise of the Lord
    Join to confirm the wondrous grace;
Eternal power performs the word,
    And fills all heaven with endless praise.

3 Amidst temptations sharp and long,
    My soul to this dear refuge flies;
Hope is my anchor, firm and strong,
    While tempests blow, and billows rise.

4 The Gospel bears my spirit up;
    A faithful and unchanging God
Lays the foundation for my hope,
    In oaths, and promises, and blood.

HYMN 64.—L. M. 6 l.

1 GREAT God of wonders, all thy ways
    Are worthy of thyself—divine;
But the bright glories of thy grace
    Beyond thine other wonders shine.
Who is a pardoning God like thee?
Or who has grace so rich and free?

2 Such deep transgressions to forgive,
    Such guilty daring worms to spare,—
This is thy grand prerogative,
    And in this honor none shall share,
Is there a pardoning God like thee?
Or is there grace so rich and free?

3 Pardon—from an insulted God!
    Pardon—for sins of deepest dye!
Pardon—bestow'd through Jesus' blood!
    Pardon—that brings the rebel nigh.
Where is the pardoning God like thee?
Or where the grace so rich and free?

4 O, for this glorious, matchless love—
    This godlike miracle of grace—
Teach mortal tongues, like those above,
    To raise this song of lofty praise!
Who is a pardoning God like thee?
Or who has grace so rich and free?

HYMN 65.—C. M.

1 Faithful, O Lord, thy mercies are;
    A rock that cannot move;
A thousand promises declare
    Thy constancy of love.

2 Thou waitest to be gracious still;
    Thou dost with sinners bear,
That, saved, we may thy goodness feel,
    And all thy grace declare.

3 Its streams the whole creation reach,
    So plenteous is the store;
Enough for all, enough for each;
    Enough for evermore.

4 Throughout the universe it reigns;
    It stands forever sure;
And while thy truth, O God, remains,
    Thy goodness shall endure.

HYMN 66.—P. M.

1 For Him who did salvation bring,
Wake ev'ry tuneful power, and sing
    To God a song of praise:
His grace diffuses, as the rains
Crown nature's flow'ry hills and plains,
    And spread a thousand ways.

2 Salvation is the noblest song,
O may it dwell on ev'ry tongue,
And all repeat, Amen!
The Lord will come from heav'n to earth
To give his people second birth,
And make them one again.

3 We see redemption drawing near;
We soon in glory shall appear,
And be forever blest;
His promise never can delay,
Our Jesus, on th' appointed day,
Will give his people rest.

HYMN 67.—C. M.

1 Father, how wide thy glory shines!
How high thy wonders rise;
Known through the earth by thousand signs,
By thousands through the skies.

2 These mighty orbs proclaim thy power,
Their motion speaks thy skill;
And, on the wings of ev'ry hour,
We read thy patience still.

3 Part of thy name most glorious stands
On all thy creatures writ;
They show the labors of thy hands,
The impress of thy feet.

4 But when we view thy grand design
To save rebellious worms,
Where justice and compassion join
In their divinest forms.

5 Our thoughts are lost in rev'rent awe,
    We love and we adore;
  The brightest angel never saw
    So much of God before.

6 Here thy great name appears complete,
    And thought can never trace
  Which of the glories brighter shine—
    The justice or the grace!

7 Though language fails, we must proclaim
    Jehovah's wondrous ways,
  And through eternity the same,
    Shall be our theme of praise.

HYMN 68.—8's & 7's.

1 O thou Fount of ev'ry blessing!
    Tune my heart to sing thy praise;
  Streams of mercy never ceasing,
    Call for songs of loudest praise.

2 Teach me ever to adore thee,
    May I still thy goodness prove,
  While the hope of endless glory
    Fills my heart with joy and love.

3 Here I'll raise my Ebenezer,
    Hither by thy help I've come,
  And I hope, by thy good pleasure,
    Safely to arrive at home.

4 Jesus sought me when a stranger,
    Wand'ring from thy fold, O God!
  He, to rescue me from danger,
    Interposed his precious blood!

5 O! to grace how great a debtor,
  Daily I'm constrain'd to be!
Let thy love, Lord, like a fetter
  Bind me closer still to thee!

HYMN 69.—L. M.

1 Immortal God, on thee we call,
The great Original of all!
Through thee we are, to thee we tend,
Our sure support, our glorious end.

2 We praise that wise mysterious grace,
That pitied our revolted race,
And Jesus, our great cov'nant head,
The Captain of Salvation made.

3 Thy justice and thy love were seen,
In thy great sacrifice for sin;
When thy dear Son, th' atoning Lamb,
Was offer'd up for guilty man.

4 A scene of wonders here we see,
Worthy thy Son, and worthy Thee;
And while this theme employs our tongues,
All heav'n unites its sweetest songs.

HYMN 70.—C. M.

1 Great God! wert thou extreme to mark
  The deeds we do amiss,
Before thy presence who could stand?
  Who claim thy promised bliss?
But, O! all merciful and just,
  Thy love surpasseth thought;
A gracious Savior has appear'd,
  And peace and pardon brought.

2 Thy servants in the temple watch'd
    The dawning of the day,
Impatient with its earliest beams
    Their holy vows to pay ;
And chosen saints far off beheld
    . That great and glorious morn,
When the glad day-spring from on high
    Auspiciously should dawn.

3 On us the Sun of Righteousness
    Its brightest beams hath pour'd:
With grateful hearts and holy zeal,
    Lord, be thy love adored ;
And let us look with joyful hope
    To that more glorious day,
Before whose brightness, sin and death,
    And grief, shall flee away.

HYMN 71.—C. M.

1 Songs of immortal praise belong
    To my almighty God ;
He has my heart, and he my tongue,
    To spread his name abroad.

2 How great the works his hand hath wrought!
    How glorious in our sight !
And men in every age have sought
    His wonders with delight.

3 How most exact is nature's frame !
    How wise th' eternal mind !
His counsels never change the scheme
    Which his first thoughts designed.

4 Nature, and time, and earth, and skies,
   Thy heavenly skill proclaim;
What shall we do to make us wise,
   But learn to read thy name?

5 Yet in redemption's wondrous plan,
   (That scheme of love divine,)
Our minds a nobler wisdom scan,
   For here our hearts incline.

6 To fear thy power, to trust thy grace,
   Is our divinest skill;
And he's the wisest of our race
   Who best obeys thy will.

HYMN 72.—P. M.

1 Thou hast, O God, provided,
   A Savior in thy Son,
In whom thy soul delighted,
   Who all thy will hath done;
And by the costly treasure
   Thy bosom freely gave,
Thine own pure love we measure,
   Thy willing mind to save.

2 O God, our gracious Father,
   Our one unchanging claim,
Our brightest hopes we gather
   From Christ's most precious name.
And that which sounds so sweetly
   In thy most holy ear,
May well our souls completely
   Relieve from guilty fear.

3 The trembling sinner feareth
   God will not all forget,

But Christ's assurance cleareth
  And cancels all our debt.
'T is doubt his heart that paineth,
  Then can we him thus grieve?
Since he full love retaineth
  Let us that love receive.

HYMN 73.—L. M. 6 l.

1 ALMIGHTY God, through Christ thy Son,
    And by thy Spirit's quick'ning power,
  We, now thy sons, in hope rejoice,
    And wait the resurrection hour:
  Redeem'd by blood, in Christ brought nigh,
  We worship thee, the Lord most high.

2 Almighty God, thy name we praise,
    Through Christ our Lord, the future king;
  We worship thee our Father, God;
    Thy love in sacred hymns we sing;
  To thee, with joy, we have access,
  Through Jesus Christ our righteousness.

HYMN 74.—7's.

1 GOD of mercy! God of love!
  Freely thou dost guilt remove,
  From the humble contrite breast,
  Seeking from thee peace and rest.

2 We adore thy matchless grace,
  Shining full in Jesus' face:
  Here we see the Mercy-Seat,
  Here we feel we may retreat.

3 Jesus came to tell of love,—
  Free forgiveness from above;
  Not to quench incensed ire
  In the bless'd Eternal Sire.

4 Mercy does no hindrance find
  In her course to human kind:
  Mercy full and freely flows
  To the heart that seeks repose.

5 'Tis unto thy mercy's praise
  We are drawn from error's ways;
  'Tis since mercy has appear'd,
  God, in Christ, again is fear'd.

HYMN 75.—L. M.

1 Come let us raise a joyful song,
  And praise the Lord with heart and tongue;
  Hosanna to th' eternal God!
  His glory let us sound abroad.

2 See how it shines in Jesus' face!
  There we behold the Father's grace;
  God, in the gift of Christ his Son,
  His utmost love to us makes known.

3 For us was Jesus made a curse;
  He died and rose again for us,
  And now for us he lives in heaven;
  Eternal praise to him be given.

4 Lord Jesus! thy return we stay,
  We long for our redemption day;
  When we thy glorious face shall see,
  And put on immortality.

HYMN 76.—7's.

1 Glory be to God on high!
Raise, ye saints, your songs of joy;
Sing the news of pardon'd sin,
Peace on earth, good-will to men.

2 Hail! by all the saints adored!
Hail! thou everlasting Lord!
Thee with thankful hearts we praise,
God of glory and of grace.

3 Christ our Savior we confess,
Christ the Lord our righteousness;
He, the Lamb of God, was slain,
And we through his blood are clean.

4 Reconciled by him to God,
We proclaim his love aloud;
And with boldness drawing nigh,
Now we "Abba, Father," cry.

5 Lord, we stand before thy throne,
Glorying in thyself alone;
Ever be thy name adored,
Holy, holy, holy Lord!

HYMN 77—S. M.

1 Raise your triumphant songs
To praise the Lord alone;
Resound, ye saints, the mighty deeds
The God of grace has done.

2 His tender mercies sing,
Who his beloved chose,
And bade him raise us from the depths
Of darkness, guilt, and woes.

3 No thunders Jesus bears;
   No terrors, wrath, or curse:
 Not to condemn, but save our souls,
   He came to dwell with us.

4 'T was mercy mov'd our God
   To send his only Son;
 Pardon, and peace, and life to give,
   And access to his throne.

HYMN 78.—C. M.

1 Behold, salvation in the Lord,
   For wretched, dying men;
 The Savior's love has writ the word,
   With mercy's blood-dipp'd pen.

2 His word of gospel grace is strong,
   As that which built the skies:
 The voice which roll'd the stars along
   Spoke all the promises.

3 He said, "let the wide heav'n be spread;"
   And heav'n was stretch'd abroad:
 "Abram, I'll be thy God," he said;
   And he was Abram's God.

4 Thy promise, Lord, supports our hope:
   Thy love our love constrains;
 Thy bounties bring obedience up;
   Thy life our life sustains.

HYMN 79.—C. M.

1 O God, all-holy, good, and just!
   Thy mercy we adore,
 And on thy faithful promise trust,
   Depending on thy pow'r.

FOR REDEMPTION.

2 When deep depress'd before thy face,
   Or with despondence tried,
We call to mind thy love and grace
   In Jesus crucified.

3 His truth and grace our fears control,
   And life and light impart;
Delightsome to the sadden'd soul,
   And healing to the heart.

4 Our life's best praise, O, God, be thine,
   For this effulgent ray,
Sent from thy glorious light to shine,
   And turn our gloom to day.

HYMN 80.—P. M.

1 O BOUNDLESS Goodness! Goodness all sustaining,
   Fain would we worship, and with songs adore thee;
O'er thy vast works we see thy spirit reigning,
      In peerless glory.

2 Heaven with praises evermore is ringing: [dor,
   While angel-choirs, o'erwhelmed with bliss and splen-
Eternal love on golden harps are singing,
      What shall we render?

3 How sweet the music of thy varied voices,
   Whisp'ring in breezes, or in thunders pealing!
Each trusting spirit in these sounds rejoices,
      Thy presence feeling.

4 Soon all our race, of every tribe and nation,
   Thy truth confessing, shall bow down before thee,
Then, then shall burst from thy redeem'd creation,
      Anthems of glory.

HYMN 81.—C. M.

1 AMID the splendors of the sun,
   Great God! thy love appears,

In the soft radiance of the moon,
  Among a thousand stars.

2 Nature, through all her ample round,
    Thy boundless power proclaims;
  And in melodious accents speaks
    The goodness of thy name.

3 Thy justice, holiness and truth,
    Our solemn awe excite;
  But the sweet charms of sov'reign grace
    O'erpower us with delight.

4 In all thy doctrine and commands—
    Thy counsels and designs—
  In every work thy hands have framed,
    Thy love supremely shines.

5 Angels and men, the news proclaim,
    Through earth and heaven above,
  The joyful, all-transporting news,
    That God, the Lord, is love.

HYMN 82.—C. M.

1 Sweet is the memory of thy grace,
    My God, my heavenly King;
  Let age to age thy righteousness
    In songs of glory sing.

2 God reigns on high, but ne'er confines
    His goodness to the skies;
  Through all the earth his bounty shines,
    And every want supplies.

3 How kind are thy compassions, Lord!
    How slow thy anger moves!

FOR REDEMPTION.

But soon he sends his pard'ning word
  To cheer the souls he loves.

4 Sweet is the mem'ry of thy grace,
  My God, my heavenly King;
Let age to age thy righteousness
  In songs of glory sing.

HYMN 83.—C. M.

1 YE humble souls, approach your God
    With songs of sacred praise;
  For he is good, supremely good,
    And kind are all his ways.

2 All nature owns his guardian care;
    In him we live and move;
  But nobler benefits declare
    The wonders of his love.

3 He gave his Son, his only Son,
    To ransom rebel worms;
  'T is here he makes his goodness known
    In its diviner forms.

4 To this dear refuge, Lord, we come,
    'T is here our hope relies;—
  A safe defence, a peaceful home,
    When storms of trouble rise.

HYMN 84.—H. M.

1 GIVE thanks to God most high,
    The universal Lord;
  The sov'reign King of kings;
    And be his grace adored.
  His power and grace   And let his name
  Are still the same;   Have endless praise.

2 How mighty is his hand!
    What wonders hath he done!
  He form'd the earth and seas,
    And spread the heavens alone.
Thy mercy, Lord, | And ever sure
Shall still endure; | Abides thy word.

3 He sent his only Son
    To save us from our woe,
  From darkness, sin, and death,
    And every hurtful foe.
His power and grace | And let his name
Are still the same; | Have endless praise.

4 Give thanks aloud to God,
    To God, the Heavenly King;
  And let the spacious earth
    His works of glory sing.
Thy mercy, Lord, | And ever sure
Shall still endure; | Abides thy word.

HYMN 85.—s. m.

1 Thy name, Almighty Lord!
    Shall sound through distant lands;
  Great is thy grace, and sure thy word,
    Thy truth for ever stands.

2 Far be thine honor spread,
    And long thy praise endure,
  Till morning light and evening shade
    Shall be exchang'd no more.

PART III.---SONGS.

SONG 1.—C. M.

1 Hark, the glad sound! the Savior comes!
  The Savior promised long;
 Let every heart prepare a throne,
  And every voice a song.

2 He comes, the pris'ners to release,
  In Satan's bondage held;
 The gates of brass before him burst,
  The iron fetters yield.

3 He comes, from thickest films of vice
  To clear the mental ray;
 And on the eyes oppress'd with night,
  To pour celestial day.

4 He comes, the broken heart to bind,
  The bleeding soul to cure,
 And with the treasures of his grace,
  T' enrich the humble poor.

5 Our glad hosannas, Prince of Peace,
  Thy welcome shall proclaim,
 And heaven's eternal arches ring
  With thy beloved name.

SONG 2.—8's & 7's.

1 Hark! what mean those holy voices,
 Sweetly sounding through the skies?
Lo! th' angelic host rejoices;
 Heavenly hallelujahs rise.

2 Listen to the wondrous story,
 Which they chant in hymns of joy,
"Glory in the highest, glory!
 Glory be to God most high!

3 "Peace on earth, good-will from heaven,
 Reaching far as man is found:
Souls redeem'd, and sins forgiven:—
 Loud our golden harps shall sound.

4 "Christ is born, the great Anointed;
 Heaven and earth his praises sing!
O, receive whom God appointed,
 For your Prophet, Priest, and King."

5 Let us learn the wondrous story
 Of our great Redeemer's birth;
Spread the brightness of his glory,
 Till it cover all the earth.

SONG 3.—C. M.

1 Calm on the list'ning ear of night
 Come heaven's melodious strains,
Where wild Judea stretches far
 Her silver-mantled plains.

2 Celestial choirs from courts above
 Shed sacred glories there;

And angels with their sparkling lyres,
   Make music on the air.

3 The answ'ring hills of Palestine
   Sends back the glad reply;
  And greet, from all their holy heights,
   The day-spring from on high.

4 O'er the blue depths of Galilee
   There comes a holier calm,
  And Sharon waves, in solemn praise,
   Her silent groves of palm.

5 "Glory to God!" the sounding skies
   Loud with their anthems ring;
  "Peace to the earth, good-will to men,
   From heaven's Eternal King!"

SONG 4.—C. M.

1 While shepherds watch'd their flocks by night,
   All seated on the ground,
  The angel of the Lord came down,
   And glory shone around.

2 "Fear not," said he, (for mighty dread
   Had seized their troubled mind;)
  "Glad tidings of great joy I bring,
   To you and all mankind.

3 To you, in David's town, this day
   Is born, of David's line,
  The Savior, who is Christ our Lord;
   And this shall be the sign:

4 The heavenly babe you there shall find
   To human view display'd,

MESSIAH—

All meanly wrapped in swathing bands,
    And in a manger laid."
5 Thus spake the seraph; and forthwith
    Appear'd a shining throng
Of angels, praising God on high,
    Who thus address'd their song.
6 " All glory be to God on high,
    And to the earth be peace;
Good-will henceforth, from heaven to men,
    Begin and never cease!"

SONG 5.—8's, 6's & 5's.

1 LIFT up your heads in joyful hope;
    Salute the happy morn;
        Each heavenly power
        Proclaims the glad hour;
Lo! Jesus the Savior is born!
2 All glory be to God on high:
    To him all praise is due;
        The promise is sealed
        The Savior's reveal'd,
And proves that the record is true.
3 Let joy around like rivers flow;
    Flow on, and still increase;
        Spread o'er the glad earth,
        At Immanuel's birth;
For heaven and earth are at peace.
4 Now the good-will of God is shown
    Towards Adam's helpless race;
        Messiah is come,
        To ransom his own,
To save them by infinite grace.

SONG 6.—L. M.

1 The lands that long in darkness lay,
    Now have beheld a glorious light;
  Nations that sat in death's cold shade,
    Are blest with beams divinely bright.

2 The great Messiah now is born:
    Behold th' expected child appears!
  What shall his names or titles be?
    The "Wonderful," the "Counsellor."

3 The Son of David and his Lord,
    Shall be the Savior of our race:
  He shall be called "the Mighty God,
    Sire of the Age, and Prince of Peace!"

4 The government of earth and seas
    Upon his shoulders shall be laid,
  His wide dominion shall increase,
    And worship to his name be paid.

5 Jesus, the holy child, shall sit
    High on his father David's throne:
  Shall crush his foes beneath his feet,
    And reign to ages yet unknown.

SONG 7.—C. M.

1 The race that long in darkness sat
    Have seen a glorious Light;
  The people dwell in day, who dwelt
    In death's surrounding night.

2 To hail the rise of that bright Sun!
    The gathering nations come,

Joyous, as when the reapers bear
The harvest treasure home.

3 To us a Child of hope is born,
To us a Son is given;
Him shall the tribes of earth obey,
Him all the hosts of heaven.

4 His name shall be the Prince of peace,
For evermore adored,
The Wonderful, the Counsellor,
The great and mighty Lord.

5 His power, increasing, still shall spread;
His reign no end shall know :
Justice shall guard his throne around,
And peace abroad shall flow.

SONG 8.—c. m.

1 See, from on high, a light divine
On Jesus' head descend;
And hear the sacred voice from heaven
That bids us all attend.

2 "This is my well-beloved Son,"
Proclaim'd the voice divine;
"Hear him," his heavenly Father said,
"For all his words are mine."

3 His mission thus confirm'd from heaven,
The great Messiah came;
And heavenly wisdom show'd to man
In God his Father's name.

SONG 9.—s. m.

1 The law by Moses came;
But peace, and truth, and love,

Were brought by Christ, a nobler name,
    Descending from above.

2 Amidst the house of God
    Their diff'rent works are done;
  Moses, a faithful servant stood,
    But Christ, a faithful Son.

3 Then to his new commands
    Be strict obedience paid;
  O'er all his Father's house he stands,
    The sov'reign and the head.

4 He sits at God's right hand,
    Till all his foes submit;
  And humbly bow at his command,
    And fall beneath his feet.

5 The man who durst despise
    The law which Moses brought—
  Behold, how terribly he dies
    For his presumptuous fault!

6 But sorer vengeance falls
    On that rebellious race,
  Who hate to hear when Jesus calls,
    And dare resist his grace.

SONG 10.—S. M.

1   Behold the Prince of Peace,
      The chosen of the Lord,
  God's well-beloved Son, fulfils
      The sure prophetic word.

2   No royal pomp adorns
      This King of Righteousness;

MESSIAH—

    Meekness and patience, truth and love,
      Compose his princely dress.

3   The Spirit of the Lord,
      In rich abundance shed,
    On this great prophet gently lights,
      And rests upon his head.

4   Jesus, the light of men!
      His doctrine life imparts;
    O, may we feel its quick'ning power
      To warm and glad our hearts!

5   Cheer'd by its beams, our souls
      Shall run the heavenly way;
    The path which Christ has mark'd and trod
      Will lead to endless day.

SONG 11.—L. M.

1 What works of wisdom, power, and love
Do Jesus' high commission prove;
Attest his heaven-derived claim,
And glorify his Father's name!

2 On eyes that never saw the day
He pours the bright celestial ray;
And deafen'd ears, by him unbound,
Catch all the harmony of sound.

3 Lameness takes up its bed, and goes
Rejoicing in the strength that flows
Through every nerve; and, free from pain,
Pours forth to God the grateful strain.

4 The shatter'd mind his word restores,
And tunes afresh the mental powers;

The dead revive, to life return,
And bid affection cease to mourn.

5 Canst thou, my soul, these wonders trace,
And not admire Jehovah's grace?
Canst thou behold thy Prophet's power,
And not the God he served adore?

SONG 12.—C. M.

1 Is there on earth a nobler name
    Than Jesus to be found?
Who can assert a higher claim,
    Or more with truth abound?

2 The Son of God, adorn'd with grace,
    Commission'd from above,
He bears to our rebellious race
    The messages of love.

3 How noble were the truths he taught!
    How pure the life he led!
And shall another Lord be sought,
    And we disown our Head?

4 Ashamed of Jesus! shall we let
    Our heavenly prospects go,
And, madly, at defiance set
    The threats of future woe?

5 Forbid it, Lord! nor let us yield
    To this unworthy shame;
But each, with holy courage fill'd,
    Rejoice in Jesus' name.

MESSIAH—

SONG 13.—C. M.

1 The true Messiah now appears,
    The types are all withdrawn;
So fly the shadows and the stars
    Before the rising dawn.

2 Now smoking sweets, and bleeding lambs,
    And kids, and bullocks slain;
Incense and spice of costly names,
    Would all be burnt in vain.

3 Aaron must lay his robes away,
    His mitre and his vest,
When God's own Son assumes to be
    The off'ring and the priest.

4 He took our mortal flesh to show
    The wonders of his love;
For us he paid his life below,
    And pleads for us above.

SONG 14.—C. M.

1 How strong thine arm is, mighty God,
    Who would not fear thy name?
Jesus, how sweet thy graces are!
    Who would not love the Lamb?

2 He has done more than Moses did,
    Our Prophet and our King;
From bonds of sin he freed our souls,
    And taught our lips to sing.

3 In the Red sea, by Moses' hand,
    The Egyptian host was drown'd;

But his own blood hides all our sins,
  And guilt no more is found.

4 When through the desert Israel went,
    With manna they were fed;
  Our Lord invites us to his flesh,
    And calls it living bread.

5 Moses beheld the promised land,
    Yet never reach'd the place;
  But Christ shall bring his foll'wers home,
    To see his Father's face.

6 Then shall our love and joy be full,
    And feel a warmer flame;
  And sweeter voices tune the song
    Of Moses and the Lamb.

SONG 15.—L. M. 6 l.

1 In Jordan's tide the Baptist stands,
    Immersing the repenting Jews;
  The Son of God the rite demands,
    Nor dares the holy man refuse:
  Jesus descends beneath the wave,
  The emblem of his future grave!

2 But, lo! from yonder op'ning skies,
    What beams of dazzling glory spread!
  Dove-like the Holy Spirit flies,
    And lights on the Redeemer's head:
  Amaz'd they see the power divine
  Around the Savior's temples shine.

3 Then does the Father loud proclaim,
    In audience of the wond'ring crowd;

154 MESSIAH—

 Attend, all nations; hear the name
  His Father gave: he spoke aloud:
 "This is my well-beloved Son!
 I see well pleasd what he has done!"

SONG 16.—L. M.

1 How sweetly flow'd the gospel's sound
 From lips of gentleness and grace,
 When list'ning thousands gather'd round,
 And joy and rev'rence fill'd the place.

2 From God he came, of God he spoke;
 To God and heaven he led the way;
 Dark clouds of gloomy night he broke,
 Unveiling an immortal day.

3 "Come, wand'rers, to my Father's home;
 Come, all ye weary ones and rest:"
 Yes, sacred Teacher, we will come,
 Obey thee, love thee, and be blest!

4 Decay, then, tenements of dust!
 Pillars of earthly pride, decay!
 A nobler mansion waits the just,
 And Jesus has prepared the way.

SONG 17.—L. M.

1 Did Jesus weep? did he shed tears?
 What beauty e'en in grief appears!
 He wept, he bled, he died, for you;
 What more, ye saints, could Jesus do?

2 Enthroned above, with equal glow
 His strong affections downward flow;
 In our distress he bears a part,
 And shows a sympathising heart.

3 Still his compassions are the same,
 He knows the frailty of our frame;
 Our heaviest burdens he sustains,
 Heals all our sorrows and our pains.

4 What pity dwelt within his breast,
 Pity by flowing tears exprest!
 O may those tears our griefs remove,
 Which speak so loud a Savior's love!

SONG 18.—C. M.

1 Behold where, in a mortal form,
  Appears each grace divine;
 The virtues, all in Jesus met,
  With mildest radiance shine.

2 To spread the rays of heavenly light,
  To give the mourner joy,
 To preach glad tidings to the poor,
  Was his divine employ.

3 'Midst keen reproach and cruel scorn,
  Patient and meek he stood;
 His foes, ungrateful, sought his life;
  He labor'd for their good.

4 In the last hour of deep distress,
  Before his Father's throne,
 With soul resign'd, he bow'd and said,
  "Thy will, not mine, be done!"

5 Be Christ our pattern and our guide:
  His image may we bear;
 O, may we tread his holy steps,
  His joy and glory share!

SONG 19.—P. M.

1 Beyond where Kedron's waters flow,
Behold the suffering Savior go
   To sad Gethsemane;
His countenance is all divine,
Yet grief appears in every line.

2 He bows beneath the sins of men;
He cries to God, and cries again,
   In sad Gethsemane;
He lifts his mournful eyes above—
"My Father, can this cup remove?"

3 With gentle resignation, still,
He yielded to his Father's will,
   In sad Gethsemane;
"Behold me here, thine only Son;
And, Father, let thy will be done!"

4 The Father heard; and angels, there,
Sustain'd the Son of God in prayer,
   In sad Gethsemane;
He drank the dreadful cup of pain,
Then rose to life and joy again.

SONG 20.—L. M.

1 "Father divine!" the Savior cried,
While horrors press'd on every side,
And prostrate on the ground he lay,
"Remove this bitter cup away!

2 But if these pangs must still be borne,
Or helpless man be left forlorn,
I bow my soul before thy throne,
And say, Thy will, not mine, be done!"

3 Thus our submissive souls would bow,
And, taught by Jesus, lie as low;
Our hearts, and not our lips alone,
Would say, "Thy will, not ours, be done!"

4 Then, though like him in dust we lie,
We'll view the blissful moment nigh,
Which, from our portion in his pains,
Calls to the joy in which he reigns.

SONG 21.—L. M.

1 "Behold the Man!" how glorious he!
Before his foes he stands unawed,
And, without wrong or blasphemy,
He claims to be the Son of God.

2 "Behold the Man!" by all condemn'd,
Assaulted by a host of foes;
His person and his claims contemn'd;
A man of suff'rings and of woes.

3 "Behold the Man!" so weak he seems,
His awful word inspires no fear;
But soon must he who now blasphemes
Before his judgment-seat appear.

4 "Behold the Man!" though scorn'd below,
Is now at God's right hand above;
While angels at his footstool bow,
And all his royal claims approve.

SONG 22.—C. M.

1 Behold the Savior of mankind
Nail'd to the shameful tree!
How vast the love that him inclined
To bleed, and die for me.

2 Hark how he groans, while nature shakes,
    And earth's strong pillars bend!
The temple veil asunder breaks,
    The solid marbles rend.

3 Behold, the precious ransom's paid,
    " 'T is finish'd," Jesus cries;
See, where he bows his sacred head,
    He bows his head and dies!

4 But soon he'll break death's envious chain,
    And in full glory shine;
O Lamb of God, was ever pain,
    Was ever love like thine?

SONG 23.—8's & 7's.

1 'Twas the day when God's Anointed
Died for us the death appointed,
    Bleeding on the dreadful cross;
Day of darkness, day of terror,
Deadly fruit of ancient error,
    Nature's fall, and Eden's loss.

2 Haste, prepare the bitter chalice!
Gentile hate and Jewish malice
    Lift the royal victim high,—
Like the serpent, wonder-gifted,
Which the prophet once uplifted,—
    For a sinful world to die.

3 Conscious of the deed unholy,
Nature's pulses beat more slowly,
    And the sun his light denied;
Darkness wrapped the sacred city,
And the earth with fear and pity
    Trembled when the Just One died.

4 It is finish'd, Man of sorrows!
   From thy cross our nature borrows
      Strength to bear and conquer thus:
   And while exalted there we view thee,
   Mighty Suff'rer, draw us to thee;
      Sufferer victorious!

5 Not in vain for us uplifted,
   Man of sorrows, wonder-gifted,
      May that sacred symbol be
   Eminent amid the ages,
   Guide of heroes and of sages;
      May it guide us still to thee!

SONG 24.—L. M.

1 "'T is finish'd!"—so the Savior cried,
  And meekly bow'd his head and died;
  "'T is finish'd!"—yes, the race is run,
  The battle fought, the vict'ry won.

2 "'T is finish'd!"—all that Heaven foretold
  By prophets in the days of old;
  And truths are opened to our view,
  That kings and prophets never knew.

3 "'T is finish'd!"—Son of God, thy power
  Hath triumph'd in this awful hour;
  And yet our eyes with sorrow see
  That life to us was death to thee.

4 "'T is finish'd!"—let the joyful sound
  Be heard through all the nations round;
  "'T is finish'd!"—let the triumph rise
  And swell the chorus of the skies.

SONG 25.—L. M. 6 l.

1 O LOVE divine! what hast thou done?
  The Lamb of God hath died for me!
The Father's well-beloved Son
  Bore all my sins upon the tree;
The Lamb of God for me hath died,
My Lord, my love, is crucified.

2 Is crucified for me and you,
  To bring us, rebels, back to God;
Believe, believe, the record true,
  We all are bought with Jesus' blood;
Pardon and peace flow from his side;
My Lord, my love, is crucified.

3 Then let us sit beneath his cross,
  And gladly catch the healing stream;
All things for him account but loss,
  And give up all our hearts to him;
Of nothing speak or think beside,
My Lord, my love, is crucified.

SONG 26.—L. M.

1 HE dies! the Friend of sinners dies!
  Lo! Salem's daughters weep around;
A solemn darkness veils the skies;
  A sudden trembling shakes the ground.

2 Here's love and grief beyond degree;
  The Lord of glory dies for men!
But, lo! what sudden joys we see!
  Jesus, the dead, revives again!

3 The rising Lord forsakes the tomb;
  The tomb in vain forbids his rise;

Cherubic legions guard him home,
  And shout him welcome to the skies.

4 Break off your tears, ye saints, and tell
  What glory now to him pertains;
Sing how he'll spoil the hosts of hell,
  And lead the monster Death in chains.

5 Say, "Live for ever, wondrous King!
  Born to redeem, and strong to save;"
Then ask the monster, "Where's thy sting?"
  And "Where thy vict'ry, boasting grave?"

SONG 27.—7's.

1 MORNING breaks upon the tomb!
Jesus dissipates its gloom!
Day of triumph through the skies,
See the glorious Savior rise!

2 Christians, dry your flowing tears;
Chase those unbelieving fears;
Look on his deserted grave;
Doubt no more his power to save.

3 Ye who are of death afraid,
Triumph in the scatter'd shade;
Drive your anxious fears away.
See the place where Jesus lay.

4 So the rising sun appears,
Shedding radiance o'er the spheres;
So returning beams of light
Chase the terrors of the night.

SONG 28.—7's.

1 Christ, the Lord, is risen to-day,
Sons of men and angels say;
Raise your songs of triumph high;
Sing, ye heavens, and earth reply.

2 Love's redeeming work is done,
Fought the fight, the battle won;
Lo! our Sun's eclipse is o'er;
Lo! he sets in blood no more.

3 Vain the stone, the watch, the seal;
Christ hath burst the gates of hell;
Death in vain forbids his rise;
Christ hath open'd paradise.

4 Soar we now where Christ hath led,
Foll'wing our exalted Head:
Made like him, like him we rise;
Ours the cross, the grave, the prize.

SONG 29.—C. L. M.

1 How calm and beautiful the morn
  That gilds the sacred tomb,
Where once the Crucified was borne,
  And veil'd in midnight gloom!
O weep no more the Savior slain;
The Lord is risen—he lives again.

2 Ye mourning saints, dry every tear
  For your departed Lord,
"Behold the place—he is not there,"
  The tomb is all unbarr'd:
The gates of death were closed in vain
The Lord is risen—he lives again.

3 How tranquil now the rising day!
   'T is Jesus still appears,
A risen Lord to chase away
   Your unbelieving fears:
Oh weep no more your comforts slain,
The Lord is risen—he lives again.

4 And when the shades of evening fall,
   When life's last hour draws nigh,
If Jesus shines upon the soul,
   How blissful then to die!
Since he has risen that once was slain,
Ye die in Christ to live again.

SONG 30.—7's.

1 Songs of praise the angels sang,
Heaven with hallelujahs rang,
When Jehovah's work begun,
When he spake and it was done.

2 Songs of praise awoke the morn,
When the Prince of peace was born;
Songs of praise arose, when he
Captive led captivity.

3 Heaven and earth must pass away,
Songs of praise shall crown that day;
God will make new heavens and earth,
Songs of praise shall hail their birth.

4 And shall man alone be dumb,
Till that glorious kingdom come?
No! the church is call'd to raise
Psalms and hymns and songs of praise.

SONG 31.—C. M.

1 Ye humble souls, that seek the Lord,
  Cast all your fears away;
 Draw near, and with delight behold
  The place where Jesus lay.

2 Thus low the Lord of life was brought;
  'T was love that brought him low;
 Thus low in death the Savior lay,
  Who lived and bled for you.

3 If ye have wept at yonder cross,
  And still your sorrows raise,
 Stoop down and view the vanquish'd grave,
  And wipe your weeping eyes.

4 Your Savior lives, forever lives!
  Raise a triumphant strain;
 No powers of hell, no bars of death,
  The Conq'ror could detain.

5 Exalted in the heavens he sits
  Though once among the dead;
 And in the future age shall reign
  Creation's glorious Head.

6 Ye mourning souls! rejoice, while you
  His empty tomb survey;
 As Christ arose, so you shall rise
  And reign in endless day.

SONG 32.—6's.

1 Sing praise! the tomb is void
  Where the Redeemer lay;
 Sing of our bonds destroy'd,
  Our darkness turn'd to day.

2 Weep for your dead no more;
    Friends, be of joyful cheer;
Our star moves on before,
    Our narrow path shines clear.

3 He who, so patiently,
    The crown of thorns did wear,—
He hath gone up on high;
    Our hope is with him there.

4 Now is his truth reveal'd,
    His majesty and might;
The grave has been unseal'd;
    Christ is our life and light.

5 He who for men did weep;
    Suffer, and bleed, and die,—
First-fruits of them that sleep,—
    Christ has gone up on high.

6 His vict'ry hath destroy'd
    The shafts that once could slay;
Sing praise! the tomb is void
    Where the Redeemer lay.

SONG 33.—C. M.

1 Hosanna to the Prince of light,
    Who clothed himself in clay,
Enter'd the iron gates of death,
    And tore the bars away.

2 Death is no more the king of dread,
    Since our Immanuel rose;
He took the tyrant's sting away,
    And triumph'd o'er his foes.

MESSIAH—

3 See how the Conq'ror mounts aloft,
    And to his Father flies,
With scars of honor in his flesh,
    And triumph in his eyes.

4 There our exalted Savior sits,
    And scatters blessings down;
While seraphs praise in lofty strains
    Around the eternal throne.

SONG 34.—C. M.

1 Blest be the Lord, who sent his Son
    To take our flesh and blood:
He for our lives gave up his own,
    To make our peace with God.

2 He honor'd all his Father's laws,
    Which we have disobey'd;
He bore our sins upon the cross,
    And our full ransom paid.

3 Behold him rising from the grave;
    Behold him raised on high;
He pleads his merits there, to save
    Transgressors doom'd to die.

4 Thence shall the Lord to judgment come,
    And, with a sov'reign voice,
Shall call, and break up every tomb,
    While waking saints rejoice.

5 O, may we then with joy appear
    Before the Judge's face,
And, with the bless'd assembly there,
    Sing his redeeming grace!

SONG 35.—6's & 8's.

1 Believers! shout and sing,
    And triumph evermore;
  Rejoice! your tribute bring,
    The Prince of Life adore—
Lift up your heart, lift up your voice,
With gladness great do you rejoice.

2 Jesus the victory gains,
    His character is love;
  When he had purged our stains
    He took his seat above—
Lift up your heart, lift up your voice,
With gladness great do you rejoice.

3 He sits at God's right hand,
    Till all his foes submit,
  And bow at his command,
    And fall beneath his feet—
Lift up your heart, lift up your voice,
With gladness great do you rejoice.

4 Rejoice in glorious hope,
    Jesus, the Judge, shall come,
  And raise his servants up
    To their eternal home—
We soon shall hear the archangel's voice,
The trump of God shall sound—Rejoice.

SONG 36.—P. M.

1 He who once was dead, now liveth,
    Jesus lives for evermore;
  He who full salvation giveth,
    He who all our sorrows bore:
      Hallelujah!
Praise the God whom we adore.

2 High the Conq'ror's state and glorious,
  Son of God and Son of Man;
He ascends to heav'n victorious,
  Finish'd all that he began:
    Thus to save us,
Sov'reign love's mysterious plan.

3 Tell around the wide creation
  What redeeming love hath done;
Publish full and free salvation,
  Through the blood of God's dear Son:
    Hallelujah!
Glory be to God alone.

SONG 37.—P. M.

1 'T was Jesus gave his life,
    That he might rise again,
  Endured the dreaded strife,
    And bore the bitter pain:
  He died and rose that he might be
  Author of immortality.

2   For us he bow'd his head,
      And yielded up his breath,
    For us, among the dead,
      He dwelt, the prey of death:
  He died and rose, that we might see
  The conquest of mortality.

3   For us he left the grave,
      And lives exalted high,
    First-born from death, to save
      Us from captivity:
  The Prince of life will come again,
  To raise his dead with him to reign.

4   Soon shall the promised hour
      Come to the waiting earth,
    When resurrection-power
      Shall give the saints new-birth:
    Then shall the Church, united, see
    Their Life and Immortality.

SONG 38.—L. M.

1 Our Savior lives, no more to die;
  He lives, our Head, enthroned on high,
  He lives triumphant o'er the grave;
  He ever lives to bless and save.

2 He lives to chase our darkest fears;
  He lives to wipe away our tears;
  He lives our mansion to prepare;
  He lives to bring us safely there.

3 He lives to mediate above;
  He lives that we his grace may prove;
  He lives immortal life to give;
  He lives, and therefore we shall live.

SONG 39.—P. M.

1 Lift your glad voices in triumph on high,
    For Jesus hath risen, and man shall not die;
  Vain were the terrors that gather'd around him,
    And short the dominion of death and the grave;
  He burst from the fetters of darkness that bound him,
    Resplendent in glory, to live and to save:
  Loud was the chorus of angels on high,—
  The Savior hath risen, and man shall not die.

2 Glory to God, in full anthems of joy;
    The being he gave us death cannot destroy:
  Sad were the life we may part with to-morrow,
    If tears were our birthright, and death were our end;

MESSIAH—

But Jesus hath cheer'd the dark valley of sorrow,
  And deathless, to meet him, we all shall ascend:
Lift then your voices in triumph on high,
For Jesus hath risen, and man shall not die.

SONG 40.—8's.

1 Behold, the bright morning appears,
    And Jesus revives from the grave;
  His rising removes all our fears,
    And shows him almighty to save.

2 How strong were his tears and his cries!
    The worth of his blood, how divine!
  How perfect is his sacrifice,
    Who rose, though he suffer'd for sin.

3 The man that was crowned with thorns,
    The man that on Calvary died,
  The man that bore scourging and scorns,
    Whom sinners agreed to deride—

4 Now blessed forever is made,
    And life has rewarded his pain:
  Now glory has crowned his head;
    We sing of the Lamb that was slain.

5 Believing, we share in his joy;
    By faith we partake in his rest;
  With this we can cheerfully die,
    For with him we hope to be blest.

6 We wait for his coming again,
    To raise us to honor and fame;
  This glory his saints shall obtain—
    His foes shall be clothed with shame.

SONG 41.—L. M.

1 Blest be the Father of our Lord,
  Who from the dead hath brought His Son;
 Hope to the lost is now restored,
  And everlasting glory won.

2 Scarce morning twilight had begun
  To chase the shades of night away,
 When Christ arose—unsetting sun—
  The dawn of joy's eternal day.

3 Mercy look'd down with smiling eye,
  When our Immanuel left the dead;
 Faith mark'd his bright ascent on high,
  And Hope, with gladness, raised her head.

SONG 42.—L. M.

1 When I the holy grave survey,
  Where once my Savior deign'd to lie,
 I see fulfill'd what prophets say,
  And all the power of death defy.

2 This empty tomb shall now proclaim,
  How weak the hand of conquer'd death:
 Sweet pledge that all who trust his name
  Shall rise, and draw immortal breath.

3 Jesus, once number'd with the dead,
  Unseals his eyes to sleep no more;
 And ever lives their cause to plead,
  For whom the pains of death he bore.

4 Thy risen Lord, my soul, behold!
  See the rich diadem he wears!
 Thou too shalt bear the harp of gold—
  And crown of joy, when he appears.

5 Though in the dust I lay my head,
    Yet, gracious God! Thou wilt not leave
My flesh for ever with the dead,
    Nor lose Thy children in the grave.

SONG 43.—C. M.

1 Triumphant, Christ ascends on high,
    The glorious work's complete;
Sin, death, and hell, low vanquish'd lie,
    Beneath his awful feet.

2 There, with resplendent glory crown'd,
    Our Conq'ring Lord remains;
His praise the heavenly choirs resound,
    In their immortal strains.

3 Amid the splendors of his throne,
    Unchanging love appears;
The names he purchased for his own
    Still on his heart he bears.

4 O, the rich depths of love divine!
    Of bliss, a boundless store:
Dear Savior, let me call thee mine;
    I can not wish for more.

5 On thee alone, my hope relies;
    Beneath thy cross I fall;
My Lord, my Life, my Sacrifice,
    My Savior, and my All.

SONG 44.—C. M.

1 With joy we meditate the grace
    Of our High Priest above;
His heart is made of tenderness,
    His bowels melt with love.

2 Touch'd with a sympathy within,
   He knows our feeble frame;
 He knows what sore temptations mean,
   For he hath felt the same.

3 He, in the days of feeble flesh,
   Pour'd out strong cries and tears,
 And in his measure feels afresh
   What ev'ry member bears.

4 He'll never quench the smoking flax
   But raise it to a flame;
 The bruised reed he never breaks,
   Nor scorns the meanest name.

5 Then let our humble faith address
   His mercy and his power;
 We shall obtain deliv'ring grace
   In ev'ry trying hour.

SONG 45.—C. M.

1 Now let our humble faith behold
   Our great High Priest above;
 And celebrate his constant care
   And sympathetic love.

2 Exalted to his Father's side,
   With matchless honors crown'd;
 And Lord of all th' angelic host
   Who wait the throne around.

3 The names of all the saints he bears,
   Engraven on his heart;

MESSIAH—

 Nor shall the meanest saint complain
  That he hath lost his part.

4 Those characters shall firm remain,
  Our everlasting trust,
 When gems and monuments and crowns
  Have moulder'd into dust.

SONG 46.—L. M.

1 He lives! the great Redeemer lives!
 (What joy the blest assurance gives!)
 And now, before his father, God,
 Pleads the full merit of his blood.

2 Repeated crimes awake our fears,
 And justice arm'd with frowns appears;
 But in the Savior's lovely face
 Sweet mercy smiles, and all is peace.

3 Hence, then, ye black despairing thoughts!
 Above our fears, above our faults,
 His powerful intercessions rise;
 And guilt recedes and terror dies.

4 In every dark, distressful hour,
 When sin and Satan join their power,
 Let this dear hope repel the dart,
 That Jesus bears us on his heart.

5 Great Advocate! almighty Friend!
 On him our humble hopes depend;
 Our cause can never, never fail,
 For Jesus pleads, and must prevail.

SONG 47.—L. M. 6 l.

1 When gathering clouds around I view,
And days are dark, and friends are few,
On him I lean, who not in vain
Experienced ev'ry human pain :
He feels my griefs, he sees my fears,
And counts and treasures up my tears.

2 If aught should tempt my soul to stray
From heavenly wisdom's narrow way,
To fly the good I would pursue,
Or do the ill I would not do ;
Still he who felt temptation's power
Shall guard me in that dang'rous hour.

3 When vexing thoughts within me rise,
And, sore dismay'd, my spirit dies ;
Then he who once vouchsafed to bear
The sick'ning anguish of despair,
Shall sweetly soothe, shall gently dry,
The throbbing heart, the streaming eye.

4 When sorrowing o'er some stone I bend,
Which covers all that was a friend,
And from his voice, his hand, his smile,
Divides me for a little while ;
My Savior, sees the tears I shed,
For he did weep o'er Laz'rus dead.

5 And oh ! when I have safely past
Through ev'ry conflict but the last ;
Still he will keep a watch beside
My bed of death ; for he has died :
He points me to the rising day,
And wipes the latest tear away.

SONG 48.—L. M.

1 Joy cometh! O! when shall it come
To those who in this desert roam!
To those who mourn—to those who weep—
To those who in death's bondage sleep!

2 Joy cometh! sighing, sorrowing one—
Joy cometh! with the rising sun!
Joy—holy, blessed, perfect, pure,
Joy—ever gushing, ever sure!

3 Joy cometh with the coming day!
Joy danceth on the morning's way!
Joy—like a flood of light shall roll,
And bathe the world from pole to pole.

4 Joy cometh! for the Lord shall come,
And raise the saints, and bring them home!
Then hearts and tongues shall find employ,
With songs, and everlasting joy.

SONG 49.—L. M.

1 The Lord is coming in the clouds,
Is coming with angelic crowds;
An universal shout shall rend
The air, and Jesus will descend.

2 How grand the pomp of his descent!
What glory waits on that event!
The glory which to heaven belongs
Is his, and his the angels' songs.

3 Unlike to those who nothing see
Beyond the world, those men should be
Who look for Jesus in the air,
And know that they shall meet him there.

SONG 50.—C. M.

1 Jesus will come—the Man of War!
   To triumph o'er his foes;
He'll break the proud oppressor's power,
   And end the captives' woes.

2 Jesus will come—the mighty Lord!
   Display his wondrous power;
Raise up his people from the tomb;
   To suffer death no more.

3 Jesus will come—the King of kings!
   To reign on David's throne;
The kingdom then shall be the Lord's,
   And the whole earth his own.

4 Jesus will come—the Prince of Peace!
   And fill the earth with joy;
No more shall angry warriors meet,
   Nor savage war destroy.

5 Come, blessed Jesus, Conq'ror come!
   Oh come, thou Mighty Lord!
Come, fill the earth with peace and love;
   Fulfil Jehovah's word.

SONG 51.—8's & 7's.

1 Faithful saints, behold descending,
   Jesus, Zion's rightful king!
See, bright angels him attending!
   Saints with joy begin to sing!

MESSIAH—

2 King Immortal! glad we hail thee,
　　Now has come the glorious day,
When our foes, and thine, shall fear thee,
　　Come Deliv'rer, come away.

3 Now earth's potentates shall tremble;
　　Now their tyrant-power is gone:
Let their armies all assemble,
　　Jesus' power will now be shown.

4 David's throne, so long o'erturned,
　　Now shall rise in glory bright,
Jesus, David's Son, once spurned,
　　On it shall maintain his right.

5 Now the living saints are changed,
　　Now the dead in Christ shall rise:
As before of God arranged,
　　See King Jesus in the skies.

6 Farewell sin and sorrow ever,
　　Jesus shall them both destroy:
In God's holy mountain never
　　Shall they hurt or yet annoy.

7 Now exceeding weight of glory
　　Shall displace affliction's rod,
No more pain, nor death, nor sorrow;
　　We are kings and priests to God.

8 Hallelujah to King Jesus!
　　We will praise him evermore,
He from ev'ry evil frees us;
　　We will all his name adore.

SONG 52.—P. M.

1 When the King of kings comes,
When the Lord of lords comes,
We shall have a joyful day
   When the King of kings comes;
Great Babylon is broken down,
And kingdoms once of great renown,
And saints now suff'ring wear the crown
   When the King of kings comes.

2 When the trump of God calls,
When the last of foes falls,
We shall have a joyful day
   When the King of kings comes;
O then the saints, raised from the dead
Are with the living gathered,
And all made like their glorious Head,
   When the King of kings comes.

3 When the foe's distress comes,
Then the church's "rest" comes;
We shall have a joyful day
   When the King of kings comes;
And then the new Jerusalem,
Surpassing all reports of fame,
Shines, worthy of its Maker's name,
   When the King of kings comes.

4 When the world its course has run,
When the judgment is begun,
We shall have a joyful day
   When the King of kings comes;
To see the sons of God, well known,
All spotless to their Father shown,

And Jesus all his brethren own,
　When the King of kings comes.

5 When the Conq'ror's hour comes,
When he with great power comes,
We shall have a joyful day
　When the King of kings comes;
To see all things by him restored,
And God himself alone adored
By all the saints, with one accord,
　When the King of kings comes.

SONG 53.—L. M.

1 The Savior comes, his advent 's nigh,
He soon will rend the azure sky;
Descending swift to earth again,
When God shall dwell indeed with men.

2 O happy day, when wars shall cease,
And ransom'd earth be filled with peace;
When sin and death no more shall reign,
And Eden bloom on earth again!

3 Saints, lift your heads; that day is near,
When your Redeemer shall appear,
To take the kingdom and the crown,
And make his ransom'd bride his own.

4 Shall not his people sing for joy?
Shall not the church their songs employ?
Sing, ye who will; sing while ye may,
And shout for joy th' approaching day.

SONG 54.—8's & 7's.

1 The night is wearing fast away,
　The star of light is dawning;

Sweet harbinger of that bright day,
   The fair Millennial morning.
Gloomy and dark the night has been,
   And long the way and dreary,
And sad the weeping saints are seen,
   And faint, and worn, and weary.

2 Ye mourning pilgrims, cease your tears,
   And hush each sigh of sorrow;
The light of that bright morn appears,—
   The long Sabbatic morrow.
Lift up your heads—behold from far
   A flood of splendor streaming;
It is the bright and morning star,
   In living lustre beaming!

3 And see that star-like host around
   Of angel bands, attending;
Hark! hark! the trumpet's glad'ning sound
   'Mid shouts triumphant blending.
He comes, the Bridegroom promised long;
   Go forth with joy to meet him;
And raise the new and nuptial song,
   In cheerful strains to greet him.

4 Adorn thyself, the feast prepare,
   While bridal strains are swelling;
He comes, with thee all joys to share,
   And make this earth his dwelling.
Lift up your heads—behold from far
   A flood of splendor streaming!
It is the bright and morning star,
   In living lustre beaming!

SONG 55.—11's.

1 The night is far spent, and the day is at hand:
   Already the dawn may be seen in the sky;
   Rejoice then, ye saints, 't is your Lord's command;
   Rejoice, for the coming of Jesus draws nigh.

2 What a day will that be when the Savior appears!
   How welcome to those who have shared in his cross!
   A crown incorruptible then will be theirs,
   A rich compensation for suff'ring and loss.

3 What is loss in this world when compared with that day,
   To the glory that then will from heaven be reveal'd?
   "The Savior is coming," his people may say;
   "The Lord whom we look for, our Sun and our Shield."

SONG 56.—L. M.

1 The Lord is coming! let this be
   The herald-note of Jubilee—
   And when we meet, and when we part,
   The salutation from the heart.

2 The Lord is coming! saints, rejoice!
   We soon shall hear his glorious voice,
   Majestic uttered from afar,
   As on he hastes his conq'ring car.

3 The Lord is coming! who shall stand?
   Who shall be found at his right hand?
   He that hath the white garment on
   That Christ our Righteous King hath won.

4 The Lord is coming! watch and pray!
   Watch ye, and haste unto the day,
   So shall you then escape the snare,
   And Christ's eternal glory share.

5 The Lord is coming! let this be
   The herald-note of Jubilee,
   And often as we meet and part,
   The salutation from the heart.

SONG 57.—P. M.

1 The last lovely morning, all blooming and fair,
  Is fast onward fleeting, and soon will appear;
    While the mighty trump sounds, "come, come away!"
  O, let us be ready to hail the glad day.

2 And when that bright morning in splendor shall dawn,
  Our tears will be ended, our sorrows all gone;
    While the mighty, &c.

3 The Bridegroom from glory to earth shall descend;
  Ten thousand bright angels around him attend;
    While the mighty, &c.

4 The graves will be opened, the dead will arise,
  And to the Redeemer mount up to the skies;
    While the mighty, &c.

5 The saints then immortal in glory shall reign;
  The Bride with the Bridegroom forever remain;
    While the mighty, &c.

SONG 58.—P. M.

1 Lo! he comes, with clouds descending,
    Once for favor'd sinners slain!
  Thousand thousand saints attending,
    Swell the triumph of his train!
      Hallelujah!
  Jesus comes on earth to reign!

2 Every eye will now behold him,
    Robed in glorious majesty:

MESSIAH—

Those who set at nought and sold him
 Pierced and nail'd him to the tree,
  Deeply mourning,
Shall their own Messiah see.

3 Lo! the tokens of his passion
   Still his glorious body bears;
 Cause of grateful exultation
   To his ransom'd worshippers;
    Hallelujah!
  Now the day of Christ appears.

4 Yea, Amen, let all adore thee,
   High on thine exalted throne:
 Savior, take the power and glory:
   Claim the kingdoms for thine own:
    O come quickly!
  Hallelujah! come, Lord, come!

SONG 59.—P. M.

1 Welcome sight! the Lord descending!
   Jesus to his saints appears;
 All their griefs and sorrows ending,
   Now he comes to dry their tears.
 Lo! the Savior comes to reign:
 Welcome to his waiting train.

2 Long they mourn'd their absent Master;
   Long they felt like men forlorn;
 Oft they bade the time fly faster,
   As they sigh'd for his return:
 Lo! the period comes at last;
 All their sorrows now are past.

3 Now from home no longer banish'd,
    They are going to their rest;
  Though the present state has vanish'd,
    With their Lord they shall be blest:
  Blest with him his saints shall be;
  Blest throughout eternity!

4 Happy people! grace unbounded,
    Grace alone exalts you thus;
  Be his praise then widely sounded;
    Sing for ever, "Not to us,
  Not to us be glory given;
  Glory to the God of heaven!"

SONG 60.—C. M.

1 Our Savior Christ will quickly come,
    As lightning shines on high;
  In clouds with power and glory great
    Be seen by ev'ry eye.

2 The dead will rise, the living change;
    From every land they'll come;
  And thus triumphant over death,
    Will then be gather'd home.

3 O glorious hope! if Jesus be
    Our Savior and our Friend;
  For we shall then be with our Lord,
    In joys that never end.

4 O may we wait, and watch, and pray;
    Free from tormenting fear;
  Our life be all devotedness
    Till he our Lord appear.

SONG 61.—L. M. 6 l.

1 Lo! Jesus comes with triumph crown'd,
   In dazzling robes of light array'd,
Faith views the splendor dawning round,
   Earth's fairest lustre sinks in shade.
Resound, resound in joyful strains,
Jesus the King of glory reigns;

2 How mean the tribute mortals pay;
   How cold the heart, how faint the tongue!
But, Lord, thy coronation day
   Shall tune a more exalted song;
Resounding in immortal strains,
Jesus the King of glory reigns!

3 Jesus, who vanquish'd all our foes,
   Who came to save, will reign to bless;
From him our ev'ry comfort flows,
   Life, liberty, and joy, and peace.
Resound, resound in joyful strains,
Jesus the King of glory reigns!

SONG 62.—8's & 6's.

1 Prophetic era! blissful day!
We catch its warm, inspiring ray,
   Which gleams o'er earth's wide plains:
We hail the dawn of morning light
That breaks upon the gloomy night,
   Where superstition reigns.

2 We hasten its advance to meet:
With vivid joy the sign we greet,
   That brightens in the sky,—

The peaceful sign of heavenly love,
Which like the holy mystic dove,
  Declares Messiah nigh.

3 Lo! Jesus comes in triumph now:
Before him see the mountains bow,
  And all the valleys rise:
He comes, with majesty and grace,
To sanctify the human race,
  And make divinely wise.

4 We'll aid the triumphs of our King!
The glories of his cross we'll sing,
  And shout salvation round;
Till every nation, every land,
From Greenland's shore to Afric's strand
  Shall echo back the sound.

5 Let earth commence the lofty praise;
Let heaven prolong the enraptured lays:
  Swell every tuneful lyre;
Bright seraphs! chant the immortal song
And pour the bounding notes along,
  From heaven's eternal choir.

SONG 63.—8's, 7's & 4's.

1 Lo, he cometh! countless trumpets
    Wake to life the slumb'ring dead;
  'Mid ten thousand saints and angels
    See their great exalted Head:
        Hallelujah!
    Welcome, welcome, Son of God!

2 Full of joyful expectation,
    Saints behold the Judge appear;

Truth and justice go before him ;
Now the joyful sentence hear ;
Hallelujah !
Welcome, welcome, Son of God !

3 Hear now the blessed Savior's voice
Calling you to life and joy ;
Banish all your fears and sorrows
Sin and death no more annoy ;
Hallelujah !
Welcome, welcome, happy day ;

SONG 64.—L. M.

1 The Lord will come ; the land shall quake,
The mountains to their centers shake ;
And, withering, from the vault of night
The stars withdraw their feeble light.

2 The Lord will come, but not the same
As once in lowly form he came ;
A silent Lamb to slaughter led,
The bruised, the suff'ring, and the dead.

3 The Lord will come, a dreadful form,
With wreath of flame, and robe of storm,
On cherub wings, and wings of wind,
Anointed Judge of human kind.

4 Can this be he who wont to stray
A pilgrim on the world's highway,
By power oppress'd, and mock'd by pride ?
O God ! is this the Crucified ?

5 While sinners in despair shall call,
"Rocks, hide us ! mountains, on us fall !"

HIS COMING AND REIGN.

The saints, ascending from the tomb,
Shall joyful sing, "The Lord is come!"

SONG 65.—C. M.

1 THRONED on a cloud, the Judge will come,
  Bright flames prepare his way;
Thunder and darkness, fire and storm,
  Lead on the dreadful day.

2 No more shall bold blasphemers say,
  Judgment will ne'er begin;
No more abuse his long delay
  To impudence and sin.

3 Then shall the Lord a refuge prove
  For all the poor opprest,
To save the people of his love,
  And give the weary rest.

SONG 66.—8's, 7's & 4's.

1 DAY of judgment, day of wonders,
  Hark! the trumpet's awful sound,
Louder than a thousand thunders,
  Shakes the vast creation round:
    How the summons
  Will the sinner's heart confound!

2 See the Judge, in grandeur nearing,
  Clothed in majesty divine:
You, who long for his appearing,
  Then shall say, "This God is mine:"
    Gracious Savior,
  Own me in that day for thine.

3 Then to those who have confess'd,
   Loved and served the Lord below,
He will say, " Come near, ye blessed,
   See the kingdom I bestow:
     You forever
Shall my love and glory know."

SONG 67.—L. M. 6 l.

1 Hail, blessed time of endless joy,
   When Jesus shall forever reign;
Where nothing hurtful shall annoy,
   But gladness fill the happy plain!
Free from all sin, and free from fear,
We ne'er shall sigh or shed a tear.

2 Ten thousand thousands then shall raise
   Their joyful notes, and sing this strain;
Awake the song of grateful praise
   Unto the Lamb who once was slain;
Hosannas, loud hosannas sing,
Hosannas to th' eternal King.

3 Forever there with Jesus blest,
   Shall fear no death, and feel no pain,
But there shall be in endless rest,
   Where dangers ne'er shall threat again:
For Jesus reigns, and we shall share
With him his fullest glory there.

SONG 68.—C. M.

1 Our Father high enthroned above
   With boundless glory crown'd,
Thou source of life, display thy love,
   To ev'ry nation round.

2 Oh, be thy will on earth obeyed,
    As 'tis obey'd, above ;
  And the profoundest homage paid,
    With all the joys of love !

3 Erect thine empire, gracious King,
    And spread its power abroad,
  Till all thy chosen millions sing
    The praises of their God.

SONG 69.—L. M.

1 Thy people, Lord, who trust thy word,
    And wait the smilings of thy face,
  Assemble round thy mercy-seat,
    And plead the promise of thy grace.

2 We consecrate these hours to thee,
    Thy sov'reign mercy to entreat;
  And feel some animating hope,
    We shall divine acceptance meet.

3 Hast thou not sworn to give thy Son
    To be a light to Gentile lands;
  To open the benighted eye,
    And loose the wretched prisoner's bands?

4 Hast thou not said, from sea to sea
    His vast dominions shall extend?
  That every tongue shall call him Lord,
    And every knee before him bend?

5 Now let the happy time appear,
    The time to favor Zion come:
  Send forth thy heralds far and near,
    To call thy banish'd children home.

SONG 70.—L. M.

1 THE trump of God shall soon be blown;
　　Its sound shall echo through the sky;
　And monarchs, with their marshall'd hosts,
　　Shall tremble when the Lord draws nigh,

2 Assume thy power, Immortal Lord,
　　Thou Lamb of God, who here wast slain;
　Put forth thine iron rod and rule
　　The wilful haters of thy reign.

3 The angry nations, yet rebel,
　　Against thy righteous claims and word,
　But Babylon and Antichrist
　　Shall fall before thee—glorious Lord.

SONG 71.—C. M.

1 GIRD on thy sword, illustrious King,
　　Thy glorious majesty display;
　And cause the nations to confess
　　Thy Lordship, and thy righteous sway.

2 Come with thy many diadems,
　　Come clothed with light o'er earth to reign;
　Ride forth in majesty and might,
　　And prosper till thy foes be slain.

3 Meekness, and truth, and righteousness
　　Are here despised, reviled, oppress'd;
　But these to raise and vindicate,
　　Thou art of boundless power possess'd.

SONG 72.—L. M.

1 O GLORIOUS hour! when Christ shall reign,
And make this world his wide domain;
When tribes from ev'ry land shall come,
To worship at Jerusalem.

2 Before him righteousness shall spread,
War then shall hide its loathsome head;
Swords to the plough shall then give aid,
And spears to pruning-hooks be made.

3 Love, joy, and peace He will maintain;
Of superstition break the chain;
"Be free," proclaim to ev'ry shore,
And bid oppression be no more.

4 O happy day! 't is nigh at hand,
When Israel shall regain their land;
When paradise shall be restored,
And Christ the King shall be adored.

5 His Kingdom then no end shall know,
Before him shall all nations bow;
E'en sceptics then shall own his might;
And be astonish'd at the sight.

6 The Law from Zion shall go forth,
From East to West, from South to North;
To ev'ry land it then shall reach,
Justice and judgment it shall teach.

7 The promise then shall be fulfill'd,
On which the saints of old did build;
Eternal Life will then be theirs;
With Christ and Abraham co-heirs.

8 O blessed day ! O precious hour !
 When earth shall feel thy saving power ;
 When all its truth shall comely be,—
 From crime and sorrow man be free.

9 The nations will indeed be blest ;
 No more the poor shall be opprest ;
 The needy then shall find a friend,
 For Zion's King will them defend.

SONG 73.—c. p. m.

1 His Kingdom comes ! ye saints rejoice !
 Let earth and heaven unite their voice
  To swell the lofty strain ;
 Proclaim the joyful news abroad,
 The mighty king, the glorious Lord ;
  Now comes on earth to reign.

2 High o'er the pomp of worldly state,
 On chosen Zion's lofty seat,
  Messiah sets his throne ;
 Now shall the lands confess his power,
 And all the earth his name adore,
  And serve the Lord alone.

3 Before the terrors of his face
 Let mortal man his pride abase,
  And ev'ry idol fall ;
 Prostrate be ev'ry haughty foe,
 The pomp and power of earth lie low,
  And God be all in all.

SONG 74.—7's.

1 Hark ! the song of Jubilee,
 Loud as mighty thunders roar ;

Or the fulness of the sea
  When it breaks upon the shore.

2 Hallelujah! for the Lord
    God Omnipotent shall reign;
  Hallelujah! let the word
    Echo round the earth and main.

3 Hallelujah! hark! the sound
    From the centre to the skies,
  Wakes above, beneath, around,
    All creation's harmonies.

4 See Jehovah's banner furl'd,
    Sheath'd his sword, he speaks—'t is done,
  And the kingdoms of this world
    Are the kingdoms of his Son.

5 He shall reign from pole to pole,
    With illimitable sway;
  He shall reign, when like a scroll,
    Former heavens have pass'd away.

6 Then the end—beneath his rod
    Man's last enemy shall fall;
  Hallelujah! Christ in God,
    God in Christ is all in all.

SONG 75.—L. M.

1 BRIGHT as the sun's meridian blaze,
  Vast as the blessings he surveys,
  Wide as his reign from pole to pole,
  And permanent as his control:

2 So shall Messiah's kingdom come,—
  Then sin and hell's terrific gloom,

MESSIAH—

Shall, at its brightness flee away,—
The dawn of an eternal day.

3 Then shall the heathen, fill'd with awe,
Learn the blest knowledge of his law;
And Antichrist, on ev'ry shore,
Fall from his throne to rise no more.

4 Then shall his lofty praise resound,
On Afric's shores, thro' India's ground;
And islands of the southern sea,
Shall soon his happy subjects be.

5 Then shall the Jew and Gentile meet,
In pure devotion, at his feet;
And earth shall yield him as his due,
Her fulness and her glory too.

SONG 76.—D. C. M.

1 From sea to sea, the King of kings,
  His empire shall extend;
E'en from proud Euphrates' stream,
  To earth's remotest end.
To him shall ev'ry king on earth
  His humble homage pay,
And different nations gladly join
  To own his righteous sway.

2 The mem'ry of his glorious name,
  Through endless years shall run;
His spotless fame shall shine as bright
  And lasting as the sun.
In him the nations of the world
  Shall be completely blest,
And his unbounded happiness
  By ev'ry tongue confest.

3 Then bless'd be God, the mighty Lord,
   The God whom Israel fears;
Who only wondrous in his works
   Beyond compare appears.
Let earth be with his glory fill'd
   Forever bless his name;
Whilst to his praise the list'ning world
   Their glad assent proclaim.

SONG 77.—S. M.

1 Soon righteousness shall come,
      And dwell on earth again :
   Jehovah Jesus, be the King,
      And o'er the nations reign.

2 Jesus himself shall rule,
      The world shall hear his word;
   By one bless'd name shall he be known,—
      The universal Lord.

SONG 78.—11's.

1 The earth shall rejoice in the reign of Messiah,
   The islands shall hear of his name and be glad;
His throne the wide world for its truth shall admire,
   Tho' now in thick darkness his dwelling is clad;
A fire all-consuming proceeds from his breath,
Which burns his proud foes to destruction and death.

2 The voice of his thunders shakes all the creation,
   The blaze of his brightness shines over the flood;
The earth bows with wonder and dread adoration,
   The mountains melt down at the presence of God;
The heavens in splendor his glory make known,
And have to all nations his mightiness shown.

SONG 79.—S. M.

1 Come Jesus, King of kings,
  And reign on David's throne;
 O come, and life eternal bring,
  And gather Israel home.

2 Raise Abra'm from the dead,
  Who did believe thy word;
 And for his mighty faith was made
  The friend and heir of God.

3 Gather his scatter'd seed
  From e'vry land and clime;
 And settle them in very deed
  In promised Palestine.

4 We Gentile pilgrims sigh,
  To be with Israel blest;
 The long-sought promised hour is nigh,
  Come, give thy people rest.

5 Come, great Restorer, come,
  Cleanse earth from ev'ry stain;
 Cause it, like Eden, yet to bloom;
  Come Jesus, come and reign.

SONG 80.—C. M.

1 That glorious day is drawing nigh
  When Zion's light shall come;
 She shall arise and shine on high,
  Bright as the morning sun.

2 When Zion's bleeding, conq'ring King,
  Shall sin and death destroy,
 The morning stars shall join to sing,
  And Zion shout for joy.

3 The north and south her sons resign,
    And earth's foundations rend;
    A bride adorn'd,—Jerusalem,
    Shall see her sorrows end.

4 Assembling with sweet melting strains,
    Jehovah they adore;
    Such shouts through earth's extended plains
    Were never heard before.

5 Let Satan rage and boast no more,
    Nor think his reign is long;
    Though saints are feeble, frail and poor,
    Their coming King is strong.

SONG 81.—L. M.

1 TRIUMPHANT Zion! lift thy head
   From dust and darkness and the dead!
   Tho' humbled long, awake at length,
   And gird thee with thy Savior's strength!

2 Put all thy beauteous garments on,
   And let thy excellence be known;
   Deck'd in the robes of righteousness,
   Thy glories shall the world confess.

3 No more shall foes unclean invade,
   And fill thy hallow'd walls with dread!
   No more shall hell's insulting host
   Their vict'ry and thy sorrows boast.

4 God from on high has heard thy pray'r;
   His hand thy ruin shall repair;
   Nor will thy watchful Monarch cease,
   To guard thee in eternal peace.

SONG 82.—C. M.

1 Nor King nor Prince on Judah's throne
   For many an age shall reign,
Nor beast upon her altar-stone
   A sacrifice be slain.

2 Pillar and Ephod cast away,
   And Teraphim forgot,
Lie hid, whilst Judah's children stray,
   As though such things were not.

3 But days shall come when Israel's feet
   A holier path shall tread,
And Judah's crown and hope shall meet
   Upon her holiest head.

4 Gather'd from far, her tribes shall own,
   That David's Lord and Son
Should sit a king on David's throne,
   Their last, their noblest one!

5 Blow ye the trumpet! let it sound
   Till the wide earth shall hear;
Judah her Savior-King hath found,
   And Israel's triumph's near.

SONG 83.—L. M.

1 When God descends with men to dwell,
   And all creation makes anew;
What tongue can half the wonders tell!
What eye the dazzling glories view!

2 Zion, the desolate,—again
   Shall see her lands with roses bloom;
And Carmel's mount, and Sharon's plain,
   Shall yield their spices and perfume.

3 Celestial streams shall gently flow,
    The wilderness shall joyful be,
  Lilies on parched ground shall grow,
    And gladness spring on every tree.

4 The weak be strong, the fearful bold,
    The deaf shall hear, the dumb shall sing,
  The lame shall walk, the blind behold,
    And joy through all the earth shall ring.

5 Monarchs and slaves shall meet in love;
    Old pride shall die, and meekness reign,—
  When God descends from worlds above,
    To dwell with men on earth again.

SONG 84.—S. M.

1 The morn is breaking clear,
    The night is flying fast,
  The day of righteousness is near,
    The time of sin is past.

2 Our master is at hand,
    He comes his own to save;
  He comes the kingdoms to command,
    To ransom from the grave.

3 He comes to heal and bless,
    To banish ev'ry ill;
  He comes to bring his scatter'd race,
    To Zion's holy hill.

4 Earth's high ones he'll abase,
    And bring them to the dust;
  His humble brethren he will raise
    To place, and power, and trust.

5 In him shall men be blest,
    His name shall be extoll'd,
No more shall nations be distrest,
    Nor war her deeds unfold.

6 Jehovah's mighty fame
    Shall spread from shore to shore,
The earth her jubilee shall claim,
    And troubled be no more.

SONG 85.—L. M.

1 Rise! crown'd with light, great Salem, rise!
Exalt thy head, lift up thine eyes;
See a long train thy courts adorn,
Of sons and daughters newly born.

2 See nations at thy gates attend,
And lowly in thy temple bend;
Behold them flowing to thy land,
Eager within thy gates to stand.

3 See heaven its portals wide display,
And pour on thee a flood of day;
Thy day shall shine forever bright,
For God himself shall be thy light.

4 Though Gentile thrones in smoke decay,
Their boasted glories melt away;
Firm as a rock thy power remains,
For thy great King, Messiah, reigns.

SONG 86.—L. M.

1 Long on the bending willows hung,
    O Israel, sleeps thy tuneful string!
Still mute remains thy sullen tongue,
    And Zion's song declines to sing.

2 By foreign streams no longer roam,
   Nor weeping think of Jordan's flood;
For thou shalt soon be gather'd home
   By thy forgiving, gracious God.

3 O Zion! lift thy mourning eye,
   The joys of nature rise again:
That long-expected hour is nigh:
   The Prince of Salem comes to reign.

4 He comes to cheer thy trembling heart,
   To bring thy day-star from the gloom;
To make thy cruel foes depart:—
   Then shall the bowers of Eden bloom.

SONG 87.—8's & 7's.

1 Yes! Judah's harp shall sound again!
   His Lion-banner flying;
Shall show the tyrant-world how vain,
   'T will be his arms defying.

2 As in the days of olden time,
   Recorded still in story;
That nation, now despis'd, sublime
   Shall rise on wings of glory.
         Yes! Judah's harp, &c.

3 Raise high your songs in Judah's praise,
   His warlike name resounding,
Recalling deeds of former days,
   When patriot-hearts were bounding.
         Yes! Judah's harp, &c.

4 For on Judea's plains once more,
   Her children shall be meeting;

And ne'er again with sighs deplore,
But give with joy the greeting.
   Yes! Judah's harp, &c.

SONG 88.—C. M.

1 DAUGHTER of Zion! from the dust
 Exalt thy fallen head;
Again in thy Redeemer trust;
 He calls thee from the dead.

2 Awake—awake!—put on thy strength,
 Thy beautiful array;
The day of freedom dawns at length,
 The Lord's appointed day.

3 Rebuild thy walls—thy bounds enlarge,
 And send thy heralds forth;
Say to the south,—" Give up thy charge,
 And keep not back, O north!"

SONG 89.—H. M.

1 Blow ye the trumpet, blow!
  The joyful, welcome sound!
 Let scatter'd Israel know
  To earth's remotest bound:
The year of jubilee is come,
Return, O exiled Israel, home!

2 For long in Gentile lands,
  Dejected and forlorn;
 Thy weary, mourning bands
  Have borne their cruel scorn:
But now thy jubilee is come,
Return, O banish'd Israel, home!

3   Thou long hast felt the rod
        Of chastisement for sin;
    Forsaken of thy God,
        An outcast thou hast been:
    But now His love again is shown,
    Return, O wand'ring Israel, home!

4   Messiah calls thee forth,
        Virgin of Israel, rise!
    From east, west, south, and north,
        Lift up thy wond'ring eyes!
    Come to thy long-lost Canaan, come!
    Return, possess thy ancient home!

5   On David's royal throne
        Thy Savior-king shall reign;
    His sway all nations own,
        From east to western main:
    The year of thy redemption's come,
    Return, O ransom'd Israel, home!

6   On Sharon's balmy plains
        Thou shalt in peace recline;
    And Beulah's wide domains
        Shall flow with oil and wine:
    Thy blest emancipation's come,
    Return, O favor'd Israel, home!

7   Blow ye the trumpet, blow!
        The Jubilee proclaim!
    Thy tribes shall blessing know,
        Though Jesus' mighty Name:
    The day of glad release is come,
    Return, O happy Israel, home!

SONG 90.—L. M.

1 Unto our God, on Judah's hills,
   Be songs of holy joy once more—
Let Canaan's rocks and sparkling rills,
   The King of heaven and earth adore.

2 For he will set the captive free,
   And break the proud oppressor's chain,
And from the isles of every sea
   Bring Israel to his fold again.

3 The Holy City's ruin'd spires
   And crumbling walls again shall rise;
Love shall relight her altar-fires,
   And clouds of incense sweep the skies.

4 There 'neath the fig-tree and the vine,
   Shall Judah's daughters peaceful rest;
And grey-haired fathers safe recline
   On sacred Calvary's hoary breast.

5 Those tuneful harps, that hung so long
   Upon the weeping-willow's stem,
Shall swell again old Zion's song
   Within thy gates—Jerusalem!

SONG 91.—8's & 7's.

1 Zion's King shall reign victorious,
   All the earth shall own his sway;
He will make his kingdom glorious;
   He shall reign through endless day.
What though none on earth assist him,
   God requires not help from man:
What though all the earth resist him,
   God will realize his plan.

2 Nations now from God estranged,
    Then shall see a glorious light,
Night to day shall then be changed,
    Heaven shall triumph in the sight.
See the ancient idols falling!
    Worshipp'd once, but now abhorr'd
Men on Zion's King are calling;
    Zion's King by all adored.

3 Then shall Israel long dispersed,
    Mourning, seek the Lord their God;
Look on him whom once they pierced,
    Own and kiss the chast'ning rod.
Then all Israel shall be saved,
    War and tumult then shall cease;
While the greater Son of David,
    Rules a conquer'd world in peace.

4 Mighty King, thine arm revealing,
    Now thy glorious cause maintain;
Bring the nations help and healing,
    Make them subject to thy reign.
Angels in their lofty station,
    Praise thy name, thou only wise!
And let earth, with emulation,
    Join the triumph of the skies.

SONG 92.—P. M.

1 High o'er the heaven of heavens I saw, and trembled,
O God of gods, thy robes of sacred splendor;
Thunders cherubic shouting, Holy! holy!
    Lord God Almighty!

2 Drop down, ye heavens! and pour a flood of glory;
Ye shades of death, the dawn of life approaches;
Mortals shall learn the music of thy thunders,
    Infinite Goodness!

RESTORATION OF ISRAEL

3 Rise from the dust, arrayed in godlike beauty,
O Solyma! immortal joys await thee:
See thy lost race burst from their chains of darkness,
Crown'd with salvation.

4 Nations unborn shall throng thy flaming portals;
Heaven's bright immortals shout o'er night expiring,
And hail the morn that lifts her smiling eyelids,
No more to slumber.

5 Shout, ye loud winds, the universal triumph!
Sing to the world, thy God, thy God descendeth!
Lifts his high hand, and swears, "I live for ever,"
Live, thy Redeemer!

SONG 93.—C. M.

1 THE sands of time are running fast,
   This age is near its close;
When the long night of pain and sin,
   Shall end with all its woes.

2 When from the heavenly court above,
   The Eternal Father's home;
Jesus, our Captain, and our Lord,
   Again to earth shall come.

3 From Zion then his strength he'll send,
   In righteousness abroad;
And haughty tyrants then shall feel,
   Jehovah's conq'ring rod.

4 His people Israel then shall hail,
   Him they did once disown;
And willingly acknowledge him,
   The heir to David's throne.

5 Kingdoms, Republics, Empires, then,
   Shall tremble, totter, fall;

Injustice and oppression cease,
  And freedom be to all.

6 The great Messiah then shall reign,
  God's glory fill all lands;
 Peoples and tongues shall then rejoice,
  Redeem'd from captive bands.

SONG 94.—C. M.

1 BEHOLD! the mountain of the Lord
   In latter days shall rise
  O'er mountain tops, above the hills,
   And draw the wond'ring eyes.

2 To this the joyful nations round,
   All tribes and tongues shall flow;
  " Up to the hill of God," they'll say,
  " And to his house we'll go."

3 The beams that shine from Zion's hill
   Shall lighten ev'ry land;
  The King who reigns in Salem's towers
   Shall all the world command.

4 Among the nations he shall judge;
   His judgments truth shall guide;
  His sceptre shall protect the just,
   And quell the sinner's pride.

5 No war shall rage, nor hostile strife
   Disturb those peaceful years;
  To ploughshares men shall beat their swords,
   To pruning-hooks their spears.

6 No longer host encount'ring host
   Shall crowds of slain deplore:

They'll lay the martial trumpet by,
And study war no more.

7 Come then, O house of Jacob! come
To worship at his shrine;
And, walking in the light of God,
With holy beauties shine.

SONG 95.—C. M.

1 But who shall see the glorious day,
When throned on Zion's brow,
The Lord shall rend the veil away
That blinds the nations now?

2 When earth no more beneath the fear
Of his rebuke shall lie:
When pain shall cease, and ev'ry tear
Be wiped from ev'ry eye.

3 Then, Judah, thou no more shalt mourn
Beneath the nations' chain;
Thy days of splendor shall return,
And all be new again.

4 The fount of life shall then be quaff'd
In peace by all who come;
And every wind that blows shall waft
Some long-lost exile home.

SONG 96.—11's.

1 Daughter of Zion! awake from thy sadness;
Awake! for thy foes shall oppress thee no more;
Bright o'er thy hills dawns the day-star of gladness;
Arise! for the night of thy sorrow is o'er.

2 Strong were thy foes; but the arm that subdued them,
And scatter'd their legions, was mightier far;

They fled like the chaff from the scourge that pursued them;
Vain were their steeds and their chariots of war.

3 Daughter of Zion! the power that hath saved thee,
Extoll'd with the harp and the timbrel shall be;
Shout! for the foe is destroy'd that enslaved thee,
Th' oppressor is vanquish'd, and Zion is free.

SONG 97.—L. M.

1 WHEN God fulfils his promised word,
Zion, the city of the Lord,
In all its grandeur then shall shine,
Majestic—terrible—sublime!

2 The glory of the Lord shall rest,
On her assemblies—ever blest;
For Christ, the Holy One of God,
Shall dwell in her, as his abode.

3 There he will place his glorious throne,
And kings his mighty power shall own;
There all the tribes of earth shall meet,
And spread their off'rings at his feet.

4 From thence shall living waters flow,
In copious streams to all below;
Dispensing health and life and peace,
Till sin and pain and death shall cease.

SONG 98.—10's & 11's.

1 HAIL to the brightness of Zion's glad morning!
Joy to the lands that in darkness have lain;
Hush'd be the accents of sorrow and mourning,
Zion in triumph begins her mild reign.

2 Hail to the brightness of Zion's glad morning!
Long by the prophets of Israel foretold;

Hail to the millions from bondage returning!
Gentiles and Jews the blest vision behold.

3 Lo! in the desert rich flowers are springing,
Streams ever copious are gliding along;
Loud from the mountain-tops echoes are ringing,
Wastes rise in verdure, and mingle in song.

4 See, the dead risen from land and from ocean!
Praise to Jehovah ascending on high:
Fall'n are the engines of war and commotion,
Shouts of salvation are rending the sky!

SONG 99.—L. M.

1 Jesus will come to earth again
On Zion's holy hill to reign;
Jerusalem he will restore,
And raise his saints to die no more,
  And raise his saints,
  And raise his saints,
  And raise his saints,
    To die no more,
    To die no more,
    To die no more,
And raise his saints to die no more.

2 The throne of David he'll rebuild,
His Royal house shall then be fill'd;
The nations then shall praise his name,
Who conquered death, and overcame.
  He burst the tomb, &c.,
  To die no more, &c.

3 Fair Zion thou shall rise and shine,
All clothed in glorious light divine:
To which the Gentile tribes shall come,
And kings unto thy rising sun.
  We'll rise and reign, &c.,
  To die no more, &c.

4 In glory then thy walls shall rise;
And all who did thee once despise;
Low at thy feet shall bow them down,
Fair Zion of the Holy One.
 We'll rise and reign, &c.,
  To die no more, &c.

5 By night and day thy gates shall be,
Wide open then continually;
That wealth of Gentiles men may bring,
As presents to thy glorious king.
 He'll live and reign, &c.,
  And die no more, &c.

6 No more shall desolating war,
The peace within thy borders mar;
Thy walls shall then "Salvation" be;
And thy gates "Praise" eternally.
 Then safe at home, &c.,
  We'll die no more, &c.

7 Jehovah then shall be thy light;
And God thy glory day and night:
Thy sun shall ne'er again decline;
Nor shall thy moon refuse to shine.
 Then safe at home, &c.,
  We'll die no more, &c.

8 Thy people all shall righteous be;
And God be glorified in thee;
They who as pilgrims long did roam;
Shall find in thee a glorious home.
 Then safe at home, &c.,
  We'll die no more. &c.

SONG 100.—L. M. 6 l.

1 Zion, arise, put on thy strength;
Thy glorious day has come at length;
Shake from the dust thyself, and shine
In grace and loveliness divine:
The mortal warfare now is done,
The day of triumph is begun!

2 O captive daughter! Liberty
Is now proclaim'd: cast off from thee
Thy bands; put on thy beaut'ous dress,
Thou city of God's holiness!
Defil'd no more thy streets shall be,
None but the pure shall enter thee.

3 Zion! upon the mountains see
The feet of One approaching thee:
How beautiful do they appear!
What doth this blessed one declare?
Hark to his voice, Jerusalem!
He cries aloud, "Thy God doth reign!"

4 Thy watchmen shall together sing
When God again doth Zion bring:
In that glad day of righteousness,
All shall be union and peace:
"Salvation" shall thy walls be named,
And "Praise," thy gates shall be proclaim'd.

5 Let Salem's wastes to joyful songs
Awake: to God her praise belongs!
When He his holy arm makes bare,
Earth shall behold, and nations fear:
His great salvation shall appear,
And Israel shout, "Redemption's here!"

SONG 101.—P. M.

1 Now pray we for Jerusalem,
  That early, she may be
 The holy, and the happy,
  And the gloriously free!
 Who blesseth her is blessed,
  So peace be in her walls,
 And joy in all her palaces,
  Her gardens and her halls.

2 Now pray we for Jerusalem,
  That to her soon may come,
 Messiah, the Redeemer,
  To make his people's home.
    Who blesseth, &c.

3 Now pray we for Jerusalem,
  That in her soon may dwell
 The chosen of Jehovàh,
  Whom He hath loved well.
    Who blesseth, &c.

4 Now pray we for Jerusalem,
  That shortly we may view,
 The Temple of Jehovàh
  In her be built anew,
    Who blesseth, &c.

SONG 102.—8's, 7's & 4's.

1 On the mountain's top appearing,
  Lo! the sacred herald stands!
 Welcome news to Zion bearing,
  Zion long in hostile lands:
    Mourning captive!
 God himself will loose thy bands.

2 Has thy night been long and mournful?
    Have thy friends unfaithful proved?
Have thy foes been proud and scornful,
    By thy sighs and tears unmoved?
        Cease thy mourning,
Zion still is well beloved.

3 God, thy God, will now restore thee;
    God himself appears thy friend!
All thy foes shall flee before thee;
    Here their boasts and triumphs end:
        Great deliv'rance
Zion's King vouchsafes to send.

4 Enemies no more shall trouble,
    All thy wrongs shall be redrest;
For thy shame thou shalt have double,
    In thy Maker's favor blest:
        All thy conflicts
End in everlasting rest!

SONG 103.—11's.

1 Ye people of Israel, remember the days,
When God for your fathers so wondrously wrought!
He still is a God who His glory displays,
And gladness shall yet to His people be brought.

2 Divided and peel'd as a people are ye:
The darkness of night is the noon of your day:
But gladsome and glorious your gath'ring shall be,
And sorrow and sighing shall far away flee.

3 Already the Highest outstretches His hand,
Already he calls from the height of the Heaven:
"Ye captives of Israel, return to your land,
"The land which to you by my cov'nant is given.

4 "O why are ye slow to possess it again;
"For your's never land of the stranger must be?

"Am I not Eternal, your cause to maintain,
"And bring you again from the deeps of the sea?"

5 The sign of the Highest is red in the sky,
  And pest'lence and war go before Him, and burn;
  But freedom shall be, and salvation is nigh,
  Return, O ye captives of Israel, return!

SONG 104.—L. M.

1 In many strange and Gentile lands,
    Where Jacob's scatter'd sons are driven,
  With longing eyes and lifted hands,
    They wait Messiah's sign from Heaven.

2 Thy cup of fury they have quaff'd,
    Till fainted like a weary flock,
  But heaven will soon withdraw the draught,
    And give them water from the rock.

3 What though their bodies, as the ground,
    The Assyrian long has trodden o'er,
  Zion, a captive daughter bound,
    Shall rise to know her wrongs no more.

4 The veil is passing from her eyes,
    The King of nations she shall see;
  Judea! from the dust arise!
    Thy ransom'd sons return to thee,

5 How gorgeous shall thy land appear,
    When, like the jewels of a bride;
  Thy broken bands all gather'd there,
    Shall clothe thy hills on ev'ry side!

SONG 105.—L. M.

1 On Zion's mount, as prophets taught,
    Shall shine the throne of David's Son;

The Gospel's latest triumphs brought,
: Where first its glorious course begun.

2 Gentiles and kings who her opprest,
: Shall to her gates with praise repair;
A fold of flocks shall Sharon rest,
: And cluster'd fruits in vineyards bear.

3 Then shall an Eden morn illume
: Earth's fruitful vales without a thorn;
The wilderness rejoice and bloom,
: A nation in a day be born.

4 The Lord his holy arm make bare,
: Zion! thy cheerful songs employ!
Thy robes of bridal beauty wear,
: And shout ye ransom'd race for joy!

SONG 106.—11's.

1 JERUS'LEM! Jerus'lem, the spoiler has trod,
On the hill of thy Zion, the mount of thy God;
And the tow'rs of thy city which brilliantly shone,
Are moulder'd to dust, and thy temple is gone.

2 But where are thy people, the once happy race,
The Israel of God and the pride of their place?
Go ask at their prophets and hear what they say,
For the wrath of Jehovah has forc'd them away.

3 They are driven afar 'mong the lands of the earth,
Their name is a scorn and the place of their birth;
And no more near their Zion its praises they sing,
For their land is the seat of an infidel king.

4 But yet, oh! Jerus'lem, thy tow'rs shall again,
Look proud on thy Zion, and smile o'er the plain;
And thy people shall come where the spoiler has trod,
Their city to build, and give praise to their God.

SONG 107.—L. M.

1 This age is speedily to close,
    Another age, soon to begin—
An age exempt from fears and foes,
    Unblemish'd by the tide of sin.

2 The "King of glory" then will reign—
    On Zion's mount behold his throne:
To lands afar, o'er ocean's main,
    His word is sent—his law is known.

3 In sweet submission, nations bow,
    Honor and worship Israel's King!
Messiah sits on Zion's brow,
    While many thousand harpers sing.

4 They sing a song that none can learn—
    The strain resounds through paradise,
While angel-hearts with rapture burn,
    And gazing mortals all rejoice!

5 From year to year the nations go
    With joy to keep the sacred feasts—
To Zion many people flow,
    Directed by their "kings and priests."

SONG 108.—C. M.

1 Isles of the deep, rejoice! rejoice!
    Ye ransom'd nations, sing
The praises of your Lord and God,
    The triumphs of your King.

2 He comes, and at his mighty word,
    The clouds are fleeting fast,
And o'er the land of promise, see,
    The glory breaks at last.

3 There he, upon his ancient throne,
    His pow'r and grace displays,
While Salem, with its echoing hills,
    Sends forth the voice of praise.

4 Oh, let his praises fill the earth,
    While all that dwell above,
In strains of loftier triumph still,
    Speak only of his love.

5 Sing, ye who stand before the throne;
    Ye angels prostrate fall;
Sing—for the Lord of glory reigns,
    The Christ—the heir of all.

SONG 109.—L. M.

1 Shout, for the blessed Jesus reigns,
Through distant lands his triumphs spread;
And sinners, freed from mis'ry's pains,
Own him their Savior and their head.

2 He calls his chosen from afar,
They all at Zion's gate arrive;
Those who were dead in sin before,
By sov'reign grace are made alive.

3 Gentiles and Jews his laws obey,
Nations remote their off'rings bring,
And, unconstrain'd, their homage pay
To their exalted God and King.

4 So will his empire still increase,
His word and spirit still prevail;
While angels celebrate his praise,
And saints his growing glories hail!

5 Loud hallelujahs to the Lamb,
From all below and all above;
In lofty songs exalt his name,
In songs as lasting as his love.

SONG 110.—P. M.

1 May ev'ry year but draw more near the time when strife shall cease,
And truth and love all hearts shall move to live in joy and peace.
Now sorrow reigns and earth complains,
For folly still her power maintains,
But the day shall yet appear,
When the might with the right and the truth shall be,
And come what there may to stand in the way,
That day the world shall see.

2 Let good men ne'er of truth despair, though humble efforts fail;
Oh! give not o'er until once more, the righteous cause prevail.
In vain and long, enduring wrong,
The weak may strive against the strong,
But the day shall yet appear, &c.

3 Though interest pleads that noble deeds the world will not regard,
To noble minds that duty binds, no sacrifice is hard;
The wise and true, may seem but few,
But hope has better things in view,
And the day shall yet appear, &c

SONG 111.—P. M.

1 To wait for that predicted day,
When Jesus shall his power display,
Be this our one great care;
To do his will our object here,
No toil to shun, nor danger fear,
Resolved our cross to bear.

2 What though our Lord should seem to stay,
   And sinners mock at the delay,
      We should not therefore sleep;
   "The Man," who wore the crown of thorns,
   Whose right the world denies and scorns,
      From heaven shall downward sweep.

3 Bright angels shall attend " the King,"
   And heaven with acclamations ring,
      When he descends with clouds:
   By faith we see his dazzling train,
   Which fills yon blue extended plain,
      With vast, exulting crowds.

4 With patience, then, we'll still endure;
   His word is true, his coming sure,
      With all its splendid state;
   "That day" we know can not be far,
   And, therefore, for his regal car,
      We still expecting wait.

SONG 112.—S. M.

1 Lord Jesus, come! for here
      Our path through wilds is laid;
   Watch, as for the day-spring near,
      Amid the breaking shade.

2 Lord Jesus, come! for hosts
      Meet on the battle-plain;
   Our holiest hopes seem vainest boasts,
      And tears are shed like rain.

3 Lord Jesus, come! the slave
      Still bears his heavy chains;
   Their daily bread the hungry crave,
      While teem the fruitful plains.

4 Hark! the herald voices near
    Lead on thy happier day;
Come, Lord, and our hosannas hear;
    We wait to strew thy way.

SONG 113.—.L M.

1 "A LITTLE while" our Lord shall come,
    Let us the precious hours redeem:
Our only grief to give him pain,
    Our joy to serve and follow him.
Watching and ready may we be,
As those that long their Lord to see.

2 "A little while," 't will soon be past,
    Why should we shun the promised cross,
O let us in his footsteps haste,
    Counting for him all else but loss;
O how will recompense his smile,
The suff'rings of this "little while!"

3 "A little while"—come, Savior, come!
    For thee thy Bride has tarried long;
Take thy poor weary pilgrims home,
    To sing the new eternal song;
To see thy glory, and to be
In everything conform'd to thee!

SONG 114.—P. M.

1 Though we know not of the season,
    When this age will pass away;
Yet we know the saints have reason
    To expect a glorious day,
When the Savior shall return,
And his people cease to mourn.

2 Being gather'd to the number
    Whom the Savior calls his own,
'Tis not meet that we should slumber,
    Unto whom such grace is shown;
Ever let his people's aim
Be to glorify his Name.

3 Waiting thus, our Lord's returning,
    Be it ours his word to keep;
Let our lamps be always burning,
    Let us watch, though others sleep;
We're no longer of the night,
We are children of the light.

SONG 115.—C. M.

1 Awake, ye saints, and raise your eyes,
    And raise your voices high;
Awake and praise that sovereign love
    That shows salvation nigh.

2 On all the wings of time it flies;
    Each moment brings it near;
Then welcome each declining day,
    Welcome each declining year!

3 Not many years their round shall run,
    Not many mornings rise,
Ere all its glories stand reveal'd
    To our admiring eyes.

SONG 116.—C. M.

1 How long shall that bright hour delay?
    When will our Lord appear?
We long to see the glorious day
    When Jesus will draw near.

2 We long to hear the trumpet sound,
    And see the just arise;
  We long to see our Savior crown'd,
    And meet him in the skies.

3 We wish to see our Lord descend,
    Array'd in robes of light;
  To Satan's kingdom put an end,
    And claim his proper right.

4 We long his coming to behold,
    That day of joy to see;
  Our ardent longings can't be told;
    Lord, let it quickly be.

SONG 117.—8's & 7's.

1 Gracious Father, guard thy children
    From the Foe's dustructive power;
  Save, O save them, Lord, from falling,
    In this dark and trying hour.
  Thou wilt surely prove thy people,
    All our graces must be tried;
  But thy word illumes our pathway,
    And in God we still confide.

2 We are in the time of waiting;
    Soon we shall behold our Lord,
  Wafted far away from sorrow,
    To receive our rich reward.
  Keep us, then, till his appearing,
    Pure, unspotted, from the world;
  Let thy Holy Spirit cheer us,
    Till thy banner is unfurl'd.

3 With what joyful exultation
    Shall the saints thy banner see,

When the Lord for whom we've waited,
  Shall proclaim the Jubilee :—
Freedom from this world's pollutions;
  Freedom from all sin and pain;
Freedom from the wiles of Satan,
  And from Death's destructive reign.

SONG 118.—C. M.

1 My soul is happy when I hear
    The Savior is so nigh,
  And longs to see his sign appear
    Upon the op'ning sky.

2 I love to wait, and watch, and pray,
    And trust his living Word,
  And feel the coming of that day
    No longer is deferr'd.

3 Then, waiting brethren, let us sing—
    He will not tarry long—
  And fill with joy the hours that bring
    The glory of our song.

4 Yes, he will come, no longer fear,
    Though earth and hell assail;
  His word attests the moment near,
    And that can never fail.

SONG 119.—S. M.

1 Ye servants of the Lord,
    Each in his office wait,
  Observant of his heavenly word,
    And watchful at his gate.

2 Let all your lamps be bright,
 And trim the golden flame;
Gird up your loins, as in his sight;
 His coming thus proclaim:

3 Watch, 't is your Lord's command,
 And while we speak, he 's near—
Mark the first signal of his hand,
 And ready all appear.

4 O happy servant he,
 In such a posture found!
He shall his Lord with rapture see,
 And be with honor crown'd.

SONG 120.—C. M.

1 HAIL, glorious day! ere long to dawn
 And set death's captives free;
Triumphant then will they come forth,
 With shouts of victory.

2 Glory to God, hosannah sing
 To Christ, our living Head—
He died and rose that he might bring
 His children from the dead.

3 The living saints, that patient wait,
 That do his just commands,
Will enter then the pearly gate
 Made not by human hands.

4 Eye hath not seen, nor ear hath heard,
 The joys they will behold,
When in the New Jerusalem
 They strike their harps of gold.

SONG 121.—C. P. M.

1 How happy are the little flock,
Who safe beneath their guardian Rock,
  In all commotions rest;
When wars and tumults' waves run high,
Unmoved above the storm they lie,
  And lodge in Jesus' breast.

2 The plague, and dearth, and din of war,
Our Savior's swift approach declare,
  And bid our hearts arise;
Earth's basis shook, confirms our hope;
Its cities' fall but lifts us up
  To meet him in the skies.

3 His tokens we with joy confess;
The war proclaims him Prince of Peace;
  The earthquake speaks his power;
The famine all his fulness brings;
The plague presents his healing wings,
  In that dread coming hour.

4 Whatever ills the world befall,
A pledge of endless good we call,
  A sign of Jesus near.
His chariot will not long delay;
We hear the rumbling wheels and pray,
  "Triumphant Lord, appear!"

SONG 122.—7's & 6's.

1 Ye who rise to meet the Lord—
Venture on his faithful word,
  Faint not now, for your reward
    Will be quickly given.

WAITING FOR THE MESSIAH.

Faint not, always watch and pray,
Jesus will no more delay,
Even now 't is dawn of day—
   Day-star beams from heaven.

2 Would you to the end endure?
Keep the wedding garment pure—
Claim ye still the promise sure—
   Faithful is the Lord!
Let your lamps be burning bright,
In God's word is beaming light,
Live by faith and not by sight—
   Crowns are your reward.

3 Tones of thunder, through the sky,
Angel-voices, sounding high,
Echo still the mighty cry,
   Jesus, quickly come!
Quickly he'll return again,
With his saints will come to reign,
While all heaven will shout, Amen!
   Welcome to thy throne!

4 Marriage supper now prepared,
By the guests will then be shared,
In fair righteous robes array'd,
   Like the Bridegroom-King.
Glory to Jehovah's name!
All shall shout the glad acclaim,
To the Lamb that once was slain,
   And his glory sing!

SONG 123.—S. M.

1   The Church has waited long
   Her absent Lord to see;

And still in lowliness she waits,
A friendless stranger she.

2 Age after age has gone,
Sun after sun has set,
And still in weeds of widowhood,
She weeps, a mourner yet.

3 We long to hear his voice,
To see him face to face,
To share his crown and glory then,
As now we share his grace.

4 Should not the loving Bride
The absent Bridegroom mourn?
Should she not wear the weeds of grief,
Until her Lord return?

5 The whole creation groans,
And waits to hear that voice
That shall restore her comeliness,
And make her wastes rejoice.

6 The Lord shall wipe away
The curse, the sin, the stain,
And make this blighted world of ours
A paradise again.

SONG 124.—L. M.

1 'T is by the faith of joys to come
We walk through deserts dark as night;
Till we arrive at heaven, our home,
Faith is our guide, and truth our light.

2 The want of sight faith well supplies;
It makes the pearly gates appear;
Far into distant ages pries,
And brings eternal glories near.

3 Cheerful we tread the desert through,
 While faith receives a heavenly ray,
 Though lions roar, the tempests blow,
 And rocks and dangers fill the way,

4 So Abra'm, by divine command,
 Left his own house to walk with God:
 His faith beheld the promised land,
 And fired his zeal along the road.

SONG 125.—C. M.

1 THINE oath and promise, mighty God,
 Recorded in thy Word,
 Become our hope's foundation broad,
 And surety us afford.

2 Like Abraham, the friend of God,
 Thy faithfulness we prove:
 We tread in paths the fathers trod,
 Blest with thy light and love.

3 Largely our consolation flows,
 While we expect the day
 That ends our griefs, and pains, and woes,
 And drives our fears away.

4 Let floods of mighty vengeance roll,
 And compass earth around;
 Let thunders sound from pole to pole,
 And earthquakes vast astound;

5 Let nature all convulse and shake,
 And angry nations rage:
 Thy name our hiding-place we make!
 To save thou dost engage.

SONG 126.—C. M.

1 'T is faith that purifies the heart;
　'T is faith that works by love;
It bids all sinful joys depart,
　And lifts the thoughts above.

2 This faith shall every fear control
　By its celestial power:
With holy triumph fill the soul
　In death's approaching hour.

3 By faith where'er his hand shall lead,
　The darkest path we'll tread;
By faith we'll quit these mortal shores,
　And mingle with the dead.

SONG 127.—C. M.

1 Lord, when iniquities abound,
　And blasphemy grows bold,
When faith is hardly to be found,
　And love is waxing cold,—

2 Is not Thy chariot hastening on?
　Hast thou not given the sign?
May we not trust and live upon
　A promise so divine?

3 "Yes," saith the Lord, "now will I rise,
　And make oppressors flee;
I will appear to their surprise,
　And set My servants free."

3 Thy word, like silver seven times tried,
　Through ages shall endure;
The men that in thy truth confide,
　Shall find thy promise sure.

FAITH.

SONG 128.—L. M.

1 I know that my Redeemer lives,
   He lives, and on the earth shall stand;
And though to worms my flesh he gives,
   My dust lies number'd in his hand.

2 In this reanimated clay
   I surely shall behold him near;
Shall see him in the latter day
   In all his majesty appear.

3 Mine own, and not another's eyes,
   The king shall in his beauty view;
I shall from him receive the prize,
   The starry crown to victors due.

SONG 129.—S. H. M.

1 Faith is the Christian's prop,
   Whereon his sorrows lean;
It is the substance of his hope,
   His proof of things unseen;
It is the anchor of his soul
When tempests rage and billows roll.

2 Faith is the polar star
   That guides the Christian's way,
Directs his wand'rings from afar
   To realms of endless day;
It points the course, where'er he roam,
And safely leads the pilgrim home.

3 Faith is the rainbow's form
   Hung on the brow of heaven,
The glory of the passing storm,
   The pledge of mercy given;

It is the bright, triumphal arch,
Through which the saints to glory march.

4 The faith that works by love,
And purifies the heart,
A foretaste of the joys above
To mortals can impart;
It bears us through this earthly strife,
And triumphs in immortal life.

SONG 130.—C. P. M.

1 O GLORIOUS hope of heav'nly love,
It lifts me up to things above;
It bears on eagles' wings;
It gives me now a ravished taste,
And makes me for some moments feast,
With Jesus' priests and kings.

2 Rejoicing now in earnest hope,
I stand, and from the mountain-top
See all the land below;
Rivers of milk and honey rise,
And all the fruits of paradise,
In endless plenty grow.

3 A land of corn, and wine, and oil,
Favor'd with God's peculiar smile;
With every blessing blest;
There dwells the Lord our Righteousness,
And keeps his own in perfect peace,
And everlasting rest.

4 O that I might at once go in!
Forsake this vale of grief and sin,
Henceforth the land possess:

This moment view my Savior here,
To end my sorrow and my fear,
  In perfect happiness.

SONG 131.—8's & 7's.

1 Know, my soul! thy full salvation;
  Rise o'er sin, and fear, and care,
Joy to find in ev'ry station,
  Something still to do or bear:
Think what spirit dwells within thee;
  Think what Father's smiles are thine;
Think what Jesus did to win thee;—
  Child of heaven! canst thou repine?

2 Haste thee on from grace to glory,
  Arm'd with faith and wing'd with prayer,
Heaven's eternal day 's before thee,
  God's own hand shall guide thee there:
Soon shall close thine earthly mission,
  Soon shall pass thy pilgrim-days;
Hope shall change to glad fruition,
  Faith to sight, and prayer to praise.

SONG 132—C. M.

1 There is a hope, a blessed hope,
  More precious and more bright,
Than all the joyless mockery,
  The world esteems delight.

2 There is a star, a lovely star,
  That lights the darkest gloom,
And sheds a peaceful radiance o'er
  The prospects of the tomb.

3 There is a voice, a cheering voice,
   That lifts the thoughts above,
Dispels the painful, anxious doubt,
   And whispers, "God is love."

4 That voice, aloud from Calvary's height,
   Proclaims our sins forgiven;
That star is revelation's light;
   That hope, the hope of heaven.

SONG 133.—L. M.

1 How oft have sin and Satan strove
   To rend my soul from thee, my God!
But everlasting is thy love,
   And Jesus seals it with his blood.

2 The oath and promise of the Lord,
   Join to confirm the wondrous grace;
Eternal power performs the word,
   And fills all heaven with endless praise.

3 Amidst temptations sharp and long,
   My soul to this dear refuge flies;
Hope is my anchor, firm and strong,
   While tempests blow and billows rise.

4 The gospel bears my spirits up;
   A faithful and unchanging God
Lays the foundation for my hope,
   In oaths, and promises, and blood.

SONG 134.—S. M.

1 Behold what wondrous grace,
   The father hath bestowed,
On creatures of a mortal race,
   To call them sons of God!

2 'Tis no surprising thing,
    That we should be unknown;
The Jewish world knew not their king,
    God's well beloved Son.

3 Nor doth it yet appear
    How great we shall be made;
But when we see our Savior here,
    We shall be like our Head.

4 A hope so much divine,
    May trials well endure;
May purge our souls from every sin,
    As Christ, the Lord, is pure.

SONG 135.—C. M.

1 BLESS'D be the everlasting God,
    The Father of our Lord;
Be his abounding mercy praised,
    His majesty adored.

2 When from the dead he raised his Son,
    And call'd him to the sky,
He gave us all a lively hope
    Of life, e'en though we die.

3 What though our inbred sins require
    Our flesh to see the dust;
Yet as the Lord our Savior rose,
    So all his followers must.

4 There's an inheritance divine
    Reserved against that day;
'Tis uncorrupted, undefiled,
    And cannot waste away.

5 Saints by the power of God are kept
    Till the salvation come;

We walk by faith as strangers here,
Till Christ shall call us home.

SONG 136.—S. M.

1 How wondrous is the love
  That makes us heirs of heaven!
The love that has renew'd our hearts,
  And all our guilt forgiven.

2 The saints though here unknown,
  Are princes in disguise:
Nor shall their glories be reveal'd
  Till Christ shall leave the skies.

3 Then shall they see his face,
  And in his blissful sight,
Shall with his image be adorn'd,
  And shine divinely bright.

4 Transported with this hope,
  And with these blessings crown'd;
Holy and heavenly be our lives,
  Such as our Lord's was found.

5 That hope shall not be vain
  Which operates by love;
While hourly fruits of righteousness
  Its heavenly virtue prove.

SONG 137.—C. M.

1 Faith, hope, and love now dwell on earth,
    And earth by them is blest;
  But faith and hope must yield to love,
    Of all the graces best.

2 Hope shall to full fruition rise,
    And faith be sight above;

These are the means, but this the end,
  For saints for ever love.

SONG 138.—L. M.

1 Faith, hope, and charity, these three,
  Yet is the greatest charity;
  Father of lights, these gifts impart
  To mine and every human heart.

2 Faith, that in prayer can never fail,
  Hope, that o'er doubting must prevail,
  And charity, whose name above
  Is God's own name, for God is love.

3 The morning star is lost in light,
  Faith vanishes at perfect sight,
  The rainbow passes with the storm
  And hope with sorrow's fading form.

4 But charity, serene, sublime,
  Beyond the reach of death and time,
  Like the blue sky's all-bounding space,
  Holds heaven and earth in its embrace.

SONG 139.—C. M.

1 Happy the heart where graces reign,
  Where love inspires the breast:
  Love is the brightest of the train,
  And strengthens all the rest.

2 Knowledge, alas! 't is all in vain,
  And all in vain our fear;
  Our stubborn sins will fight and reign,
  If love be absent there.

3 'T is love that makes our cheerful feet
  In swift obedience move;

The demon's know and tremble too,
  But Satan cannot love.

4 This is the grace that lives and sings,
    When faith and hope shall cease;
  'T is this shall strike our joyful strings
    In the sweet realms of bliss.

SONG 140.—L. M.

1 How blest the sacred tie, that binds
  In sweet communion kindred minds!
  How swift the heavenly course they run,
  Whose hearts, whose faith, whose hopes are one.

2 To each, the life of each how dear!
  What tender love!—what holy fear!
  How does the gen'rous flame within
  Refine from earth, and cleanse from sin!

3 Their streaming eyes together flow
  For human guilt and human woe;
  Their ardent prayers together rise,
  Like mingling flame and sacrifice.

4 Together oft they seek the place
  Where God reveals his smiling face:
  How high, and strong their raptures swell;
  There's none but kindred souls can tell.

SONG 141.—S. M.

1 Blest be the tie that binds
    Our hearts in Christian love!
  The fellowship of kindred minds
    Is like to that above.

2 Before our Father's throne
    We pour our ardent prayers;

Our fears, our hopes, our aims are one,
  Our comforts and our cares.
3 When we asunder part,
  It gives us inward pain;
But we shall still be join'd in heart,
  And hope to meet again.
4 This glorious hope revives
  Our courage by the way;
While each in expectation lives,
  And longs to see the day.
5 From sorrow, toil and pain,
  And sin we shall be free;
And perfect love and friendship reign
  Through all eternity.

SONG 142.—C. M.

1 How sweet, how heavenly is the sight
  When those that love the Lord,
In one another's peace delight,
  And thus fulfil his word!
2 When each can feel his brother's sigh,
  And with him bear a part;
When sorrow flows from eye to eye,
  And joy from heart to heart!
3 When, free from envy, scorn and pride,
  Our wishes all above,
Each can his brother's failings hide,
  And show a brother's love!
4 When love, in one delightful stream,
  Through ev'ry bosom flows;
And union sweet, and dear esteem,
  In ev'ry action glows!

P

SONG 143.—C. M.

1 Lo! what an entertaining sight
    Those friendly brethren prove,
  Whose cheerful hearts in bands unite
    Of harmony and love!

2 Where streams of bliss from Christ the spring,
    Descend on ev'ry soul;
  And heavenly peace with balmy wing
    Shades and revives the whole.

3 'T is pleasant as the morning dews
    That fall on Zion's hill,
  Where God his mildest glory shows,
    And makes his grace distill.

SONG 144.—L. M.

1 Had I the tongues of Greeks and Jews,
  And nobler speech than angels use,
  If love be absent, I am found,
  Like tinkling brass, an empty sound.

2 Were I inspired, O God, to know
  All that is done above, below,
  Or could my faith the mountains move,
  Still I am nothing without love.

3 Should I distribute all my store,
  To feed the bowels of the poor;
  Or give my body to the flame,
  To gain a martyr's glorious name;—

4 If love to God, and love to men,
  Be absent, all my hopes are vain:
  Nor tongues, nor gifts, nor fiery zeal,
  The works of love can e'er fulfil.

SONG 145.—C. M.

1 Could I with elocution speak,
    Transcending human tongue;
And could I sing in strains more sweet
    Than ever angel sung.

2 And did not charity inspire,
    And raise herself—my voice,
My flowing verse were empty sound,
    "My eloquence were noise."

3 Yea, had I faith to weary racks,
    And pass unhurt through flame;
And did not charity inspire,
    My suff'rings were in vain.

4 'Tis love which spreads the wings of hope,
    And bids her strength exert;
Which brings our faith from sound to things,
    From fancy to the heart.

5 A time shall come, when constant faith
    And patient hope shall die;
One lost in certainty of sight,
    And one dissolv'd in joy.

6 But love shall last when these no more
    Shall warm the pilgrim's breast,
Or open on his ravish'd eyes
    His long-expected rest.

7 Love's unextinguish'd ray shall burn
    Through death, unchang'd its frame:
Its lamp shall triumph o'er the grave,
    With uncorrupted flame.

SONG 146.—L. M.

1 And is the gospel peace and love?
   Such let our conversation be;
 The serpent blended with the dove,
   Wisdom and meek simplicity.

2 Whene'er the angry passions rise,
   And tempt our thoughts or tongues to strife,
 To Jesus let us lift our eyes,
   Bright pattern of the Christian-life!

3 To do his heavenly Father's will
   Was his employment and delight;
 Humility and holy zeal
   Shone through his life divinely bright.

4 Dispensing good where'er he came,
   The labors of his life were love;
 Then if we bear the Savior's name,
   By his example let us move.

5 O, how benevolent and kind!
   How mild—how ready to forgive!
 Be this the temper of our mind,
   And these the rules by which we live.

SONG 147.—L. M.

1 My blest Redeemer and my Lord,
 I read my duty in thy Word;
 But in thy life the law appears,
 Drawn out in living characters.

2 What truth and love thy bosom fill!
 What zeal to do thy Father's will!
 Such zeal, and truth, and love divine,
 I would transcribe, and make them mine.

3 Cold mountains, and the midnight air,
  Witness'd the fervor of thy prayer;
  The desert thy temptations knew,
  Thy conflict, and thy victory too.

4 Be thou my pattern; may I bear
  More of thy gracious image here;
  Then God the Judge, shall own my name
  Among the foll'wers of the Lamb.

SONG 148.—L. M.

1 So let our lips and lives express
  The holy gospel we profess;
  So let our works and virtues shine,
  To prove the doctrine all divine.

2 Thus shall we best proclaim abroad
  The honors of our Maker, God,
  When his salvation reigns within,
  And grace subdues the power of sin.

3 Our flesh and sense must be denied,
  Ambition, envy, lust, and pride;
  While justice, temp'rance, truth, and love
  Our inward piety approve.

4 Religion bears our spirits up,
  While we expect that blessed hope
  The bright appearance of the Lord,
  And faith stands leaning on his word.

SONG 149.—C. M.

1 Am I a soldier of the cross,
    A foll'wer of the Lamb?
  And shall I fear to own his cause,
    Or blush to speak his name?

2 Shall I in sloth indulge my eyes,
On flow'ry beds of ease,
While others fought to win the prize,
And sail'd thro' bloody seas?

3 Are there no foes for me to face?
Must I not stem the flood?
Is this vile world a friend to grace,
To help me on to God?

4 Sure I must fight, if I would reign!
Increase my courage, Lord!
I'll bear the toil, endure the pain,
Supported by thy word.

SONG 150.—L. M.

1 Jesus, my King, proclaims the war;
"Awake! the powers of hell are near;
To arms! to arms!" I hear him cry;
"'T is your's to conquer or to die!"

2 Roused by the animating sound,
I cast my eager eyes around;
I haste to gird my armor on,
And bid each trembling fear be gone.

3 Hope is my helmet, faith my shield;
The word of God the sword I wield;
With sacred truth my loins are girt,
And holy zeal inspires my heart.

4 Thus arm'd, I venture on the fight,
Resolved to put my foes to flight,
While Jesus kindly deigns to spread
His conq'ring banner o'er my head.

5 In him I hope, in him I trust;
His bleeding cross is all my boast;

WARFARE. 247

Through troops of foes he'll lead me on
To victory, and the victor's crown.

SONG 151.—7's & 8's.

1 CHRISTIAN soldier, seize thy sword,
  Seek the field, and take thy station!
Prince Messiah gives the word,
  Captain of the saints' salvation.

2 Strong the weapons thou must wield,
  Stern the warfare thou art waging;
Bind the helmet, bear the shield,
  Hell's beleag'ring hosts engaging.

3 Lo! the battle is begun!
  Lo! Immanuel's troops in motion!
Some the prize have nearly won,
  And they soon will seize their portion.

4 Hear you not the victor's song?
  Hear you not the captives crying?
Shout! Jehovah's arm is strong;
  Shout! the alien foe is flying.

5 See the crimson banners wave!
  Hear the chariot's rolling thunder,
Christ the conquer'd world shall save,
  Cleaving Satan's throne asunder.

6 Lo! the ransom'd marching home!
  Anthems loud and palms victorious;
Satan conquer'd, death o'ercome,
  Crowns secured and mansions glorious.

SONG 152.—L. M.

1 AWAKE, my soul! lift up thine eyes;
  See where thy foes against thee rise,

In long array, a num'rous host;
Awake, my soul! or thou art lost.

2 Here giant danger threat'ning stands,
Mustering his pale, terrific bands;
There pleasure's silken banners spread,
And willing souls are captive led.

3 See where rebellious passions rage,
And fierce desires and lusts engage;
The meanest foe of all the train
Has thousands and ten thousands slain.

4 Thou tread'st upon enchanted ground;
Perils and snares beset thee round;
Beware of all; guard every part;
But most, the traitor in thy heart.

5 Come, then, my soul! now learn to wield
The weight of thine immortal shield;
Put on the armor from above,
Of heavenly truth, and heavenly love.

6 The terror and the charm repel,
And powers of earth, and powers of hell;
The Man of Calvary triumph'd here;—
Why should his faithful foll'wers fear?

SONG 153.—7's.

1 Much in sorrow, oft in woe,
Onward, Christians, onward go;
Fight the fight; and, worn with strife,
Steep with tears the bread of life.

2 Onward, Christians, onward go;
Join the war, and face the foe;
Faint not; much doth yet remain;
Dreary is the long campaign.

3 Shrink not, Christians,—will ye yield?
Will ye quit the battle-field?
Fight till all the conflict's o'er,
Nor your foes shall rally more.

4 But when loud the trumpet blown,
Speaks their forces overthrown,
Christ, your Captain, shall bestow,
Crowns to grace the conq'ror's brow.

SONG 154.—C. M.

1 O, SPEED thee, Christian, on thy way,
    And to thy armor cling;
With girded loins the call obey
    That grace and mercy bring.

2 There is a battle to be fought,
    An upward race to run,
A crown of glory to be sought,
    A vict'ry to be won.

3 O, faint not, Christian, for thy sighs
    Are heard before His throne;
The race must come before the prize,
    The cross before the crown.

SONG 155.—C. M.

1 AWAKE, my soul! stretch every nerve,
    And press with vigor on;
A heavenly race demands thy zeal,
    And an immortal crown.

2 A cloud of witnesses around
    Hold thee in full survey;
Forget the steps already trod,
    And onward urge thy way.

3 'T is God's all-animating voice
    That calls thee from on high;
'T is his own hand presents the prize
    To thine uplifted eye;—

4 That prize, with peerless glories bright,
    Which shall new lustre boast,
When victors' wreaths and monarchs' gems
    Shall blend in common dust.

SONG 156.—P. M.

1 GUIDE us, O thou great Jehovah,
    Pilgrims through this barren land;
We are weak, but thou art mighty,
    Hold us with thy powerful hand:
      Bread of heaven,
Feed us now and evermore.

2 Fill us from the living Fountain,
    Whence the crystal waters flow;
Let the bright and cloudy pillar
    Lead us all our journey through:
      Strong Deliv'rer,
Be thou still our Sun and Shield.

3 Musing on thy great salvation,
    Musing on our heavenly home,
We exclaim with holy longing,
    "Come, Lord Jesus, quickly come:"
      Great Jehovah,
Let us soon thy glory see.

SONG 157.—L. M.

1 BROAD is the road that leads to death,
    And thousands walk together there!

But wisdom shows a narrower path,
With here and there a traveller.

2 " Deny thyself, and take thy cross,"
Is the Redeemer's great command!
Nature must count her gold but dross
If she would gain the heavenly land.

3 The fearful soul that tires and faints,
And walks the way of God no more,
Is but esteemed almost a saint,
And makes his own destruction sure.

4 Lord, let not all my hopes be vain;
Create my heart entirely new;
True holiness may I attain,
And share in endless glory too!

SONG 158.—C. M.

1 Our country is Immanuel's ground,
    We seek that promised soil;
The songs of Zion cheer our hearts,
    While strangers here we toil.

2 We tread the path our Master trod,
    We bear the cross he bore;
And every thorn that wounds our feet,
    His temples pierced before.

3 Oft do our eyes with joy o'erflow,
    And oft are bathed in tears;
Yet nought but heaven our hopes can raise,
    And nought but sin our fears.

SONG 159.—C. M.

1 Sing, ye redeemed of the Lord,
    Your great Deliverer sing;

Pilgrims for Zion's city bound,
  Be joyful in your King.
2 See the fair way his hand hath raised,
    How holy and how plain!
  Nor shall the simplest traveller err,
    Nor ask the track in vain.
3 No ravening lion shall destroy,
    Nor lurking serpent wound;
  Pleasure and safety, peace and praise,
    Through all the path are found.
4 A hand divine shall lead you on,
    Through all the blissful road;
  Till to the sacred mount you rise,
    And see your smiling God.
5 There garlands of immortal joy
    Shall bloom on every head;
  While sorrow, sighing, and distress,
    Like shadows all are fled.
6 March on in your Redeemer's strength
    Pursue his footsteps still;
  And let the prospect cheer your eye,
    While laboring up the hill.

SONG 160.—S. M.

1 THE people of the Lord
    Are on their way to heaven;
  There they obtain their great reward,
    The prize will there be given.
2 'T is conflict here below;
    'T is triumph there, and peace;
  On earth we wrestle with the foe,
    In heaven our conflicts cease.

3 There rest shall follow toil,
   And ease succeed to care;
 The victors there divide the spoil;
   They sing and triumph there.

4 Then let us joyful sing!
   The conflict is not long:
 We hope ere long to praise our King,
   In one eternal song.

SONG 161.—7's.

1 Children of the heavenly King,
 As ye journey, sweetly sing!
 Sing your Maker's worthy praise,
 Glorious in his works and ways.

2 Shout, ye ransom'd flock, and blest!
 You on Jesus' throne shall rest;
 There your seat will be prepared;
 There your kingdom and reward.

3 Fear not, brethren, joyful stand
 On the borders of your land;
 Jesus, God's exalted Son,
 Bids you undismay'd go on.

4 Lord! submissive may we go,
 Gladly leaving all below;
 Only thou our leader be,
 And we still will follow thee!

SONG 162.—11's.

1 'Mid scenes of confusion and creature complaints,
 How sweet to my soul is communion with saints,
 To find at the banquet of mercy there's room,
 And feel in the presence of Jesus at home.
   Home, home, sweet, sweet home,
 Prepare me, dear Savior, for glory, my home.

ORDINANCES—

2 Sweet bonds that unite all the children of peace,
  And thrice precious Jesus whose love cannot cease,
  Though oft from his presence in sadness I roam,
  I long to behold him in glory at home.
    Home, home, sweet, sweet home, &c.

3 I long dearest Lord, in thy beauties to shine,
  No more as an exile, in sorrow to pine,
  And in thy dear image, arise o'er the tomb,
  With glorified millions to praise thee at home.
    Home, home, sweet, sweet home,
  O take me, dear Savior, to glory, my home.

SONG 163—L. M.

1 'Twas the commission of our Lord,
    "Go teach the nations, and baptize;"
  The nations have received the word
    Since he ascended to the skies.

2 He sits upon th' eternal hills,
    With grace and pardon in his hands,
  And sends his cov'nant with the seals
    To bless the distant Gentile lands.

3 "Repent, and be immersed," he saith,
    "For the remission of your sins;"
  And thus our sense assists our faith,
    And shows us what his gospel means.

SONG 164.—C. M.

1 Witness, oh Lord, the solemn act
    Which we this day perform,
  And grant Thy blessing on the one
    Who doth his faith affirm.
  A sinner dies this day to sin,
    Is buried with his Lord,
  And rises a new life to live,
    According to thy Word.

IMMERSION. 255

2 His faith the one Thou hast ordained,
    Inheritance he claims:
  Intent salvation to attain
    For Ages-life he aims.
  He sets his seal to thy demands,
    The covenant approves,
  And shows by works of righteousness
    Thy promises he loves.

3 Born thus of water, may he grow
    In grace and truth divine
  Till when the Spirit gives new birth
    He 'll in Thy image shine.
  Accept then his obedient faith
    Do thou his sins remit ;
  And may he in the holy race
    Himself with zeal acquit.

SONG 165.—P. M.

1 Thou hast said, exalted Jesus,
    Take thy cross and follow me ;
  Shall the word with terror seize us?
    Shall we from thy burden flee?
      Lord, I'll take it,
  And rejoicing, follow thee.

2 While this liquid tomb surveying,
    Emblem of my Savior's grave,
  Shall I shun its brink, betraying
    Feelings worthy of a slave?
      No! I'll enter;
  Jesus entered Jordan's wave.

3 Blest the sign which thus reminds me,
    Savior, of thy love for me;

But more blest the love that binds me
In its deathless bonds to thee;
O what pleasure,
Buried with my Lord to be!

4 Should it rend some fond connection,
Should I suffer shame or loss,
Yet the fragrant, blest reflection,
I have been where Jesus was,
Will revive me
When I faint beneath the cross.

5 Fellowship with him possessing,
Let me die to earth and sin;
Let me rise t' enjoy the blessing
Which the faithful soul shall win:
May I ever
Follow where my Lord has been.

SONG 166.—C. M.

1 BURIED with Christ! yes, thus we lie
Immersed beneath the wave;
So he, the Savior from on high,
Found on this earth his grave.

2 We rise with him! to live anew
A holy life of faith;
Believing what this brings to view,
And what the Scripture saith—

3 The glorious resurrection morn!
When Jesus from the skies
Descending, whence he now hath gone,
Shall bid the sleeping rise.

4 Eternal life we then receive
From him our blessed Lord;

Help us, O Father, to believe,
And trust thy Holy Word.

SONG 167.—P. M.

1 " Go, preach the Gospel," said the Lord,
　Let all the nations hear ;
" He who believes" the kingdom's word,
　And turns to God with fear,
" And is immersed," shall saved be,
From sin and death he shall be free.

2 The glorious news was spread abroad,
　· On wings of joy and love ;
Till many nations heard the word,—
　That message from above ;
The news of pardon, peace, and heaven,
Through God's own Son so freely given.

3 Faith in the word which God has sent,
　Precedes the law of faith ;
" Believe the Gospel," and " repent,"
　Then " be immersed," he saith ;
Pardon of sins such souls receive,
And in the future age will live.

4 Thus in the likeness of his death
　We're buried with our Lord ;
And rise to live a life of faith,
　And feed upon his word ;
Then at the resurrection morn,
We of the Spirit shall be born.

SONG 168.—C. M.

1 If human kindness meets return,
　And owns the grateful tie ;—

ORDINANCES—

If tender thoughts within us burn
  To feel a friend is nigh;—
2 O, shall not warmer accents tell,
  The gratitude we owe
To Him who died our fears to quell,
  And save from sin and woe.

3 While yet his anguish'd soul survey'd
  Those pangs he would not flee,
What love his latest words display'd!—
  "Meet and remember me."

4 Remember thee! thy death, thy shame,
  Thy griefs which thou didst bear!
O memory, leave no other name
  But his recorded there!

SONG 169.—S. M.

1   Here, in the broken bread,
      Here, in the cup we take,
    His body and his blood behold,
      Who suffer'd for our sake.

2   Yes, that our souls might live,
      Those sacred limbs were torn,
    That blood was spilt, and pangs untold
      Were by the Savior borne.

3   O Thou who didst allow
      Thy Son to suffer thus,
    Father, what more couldst thou have done
      Than thou hast done for us?

4   We are persuaded now,
      That nothing can divide
    Thy children from thy boundless love,
      Display'd in him who died;—

SUPPER. 259

5 Who died to make us sure
  Of mercy, truth, and peace,
And from the power and pains of sin
  To bring a full release.

SONG 170.—7's.

1 Not with terror do we meet
    At the board by Jesus spread:
  Not in mystery drink and eat
    Of the Savior's wine and bread.

2 'T is his memory we record,
    'T is his virtues we proclaim;
  Grateful to our honored Lord,
    Here we bless his sacred name.

3 See him on the dreadful day
    Of his mortal agony,
  Break the bread; and hear him say,
    " Eat of this, and think of me!"

4 See him standing on the brink
    Of the tomb, and hark! he cries,
  " Drink the wine, and as you drink,
    O, remember him who dies!"

5 Yes! we will remember thee,
    Friend and Savior! and thy feast,
  Of all services shall be,
    Holiest and welcomest.

SONG 171.—C. M.

1 According to thy gracious word,
    In meek humility,
  This will we do, our dying Lord;
    We will remember thee.

2 Thy body, broken for our sake,
    Our bread from heaven shall be;
Thy testamental cup we take,
    And thus remember thee.

3 Gethsemane can we forget?
    Or there thy conflict see,
Thine agony and bloody sweat,
    And not remember thee?

4 When to the cross we turn our eyes,
    And rest on Calvary,
O Lamb of God, our sacrifice!
    We must remember thee.

5 Remember thee, and all thy pains,
    And all thy love so free!
Yea, while a breath, a pulse remains,
    Will we remember thee.

6 And when these failing lips grow dumb,
    And mind and mem'ry flee,
When thou shalt in thy glory come,
    May we remember'd be.

SONG 172.—L. M.

1 In mem'ry of our absent Lord,
    With holy love, and sacred joy,
We meet around this festive board,
    While songs of praise our tongues employ.

2 "Do this, and thus remember me,"
    To a few chosen friends, he said;
Lord, we would too remember thee,
    And own thee as our living Head.

3 Obedient to thy last request,
    We eat the bread, and drink the wine;

Thus with thy presence we are blest,
  And joy to know that we are thine.
4 In faith we eat thy mystic flesh,
    In faith we drink thy mystic blood;
  These symbols here our minds refresh,
    As life is now sustain'd by food.
5 Rememb'ring Jesus, we desire,
    A counterpart of him to be;
  To holiness of life aspire,—
    Through him obtain the victory.
6 Till his return, we thus would meet,
    And show the world his dying love;
  Then with him in his kingdom sit,
    Nor from his presence ere remove.

SONG 173.—C. M.

1 In blessed union here we meet,
  Around our great Redeemer's feet,
    To eat the bread of heaven;
  How highly privileged are we,
  And, oh, how thankful should we be,
    To whom this grace is given.
2 And if such blessedness we know,
  Amid this world of sin and woe,
    How blest we soon shall be,
  When we our Lord himself shall meet,
  And dwell in fellowship complete,
    In immortality.

SONG 174.—S. M.

1   Jesus, the friend of man,
      Invites us to his board;

The welcome summons we obey
And own our gracious Lord.

2 Here we survey that love,
Which spoke in ev'ry breath,
Prompted each action of his life
And triumph'd in his death.

3 Here let our powers unite,
His honor'd name to raise;
Let grateful joy fill ev'ry mind,
And ev'ry voice be praise.

4 One faith, one hope, one Lord,
One God alone we know;
Brethren we are; let ev'ry heart
With kind affections glow.

SONG 175.—8's & 7's.

1 In the cross of Christ I glory,
Tow'ring o'er the wrecks of time;
All the light of sacred story,
Gathers 'round its head sublime.

2 When the woes of life o'ertake me,
Hopes deceive, and fears annoy,
Never shall the cross forsake me;
Lo! it glows with peace and joy.

3 When the sun of bliss is beaming
Light and love upon my way,
From the cross the radiance streaming,
Adds new lustre to the day.

4 Bane and blessing, pain and pleasure,
By the cross are sanctified;
Peace is there that knows no measure,
Joys that through all time abide.

5 In the cross of Christ I glory,
  Tow'ring o'er the wrecks of time;
  All the light of sacred story,
  Gathers round its head sublime.

SONG 176.—L. M.

1 IF love, the noblest, purest, best,
  If truth, all other truths above,
  Will claim returns from every breast,
  Oh! surely Jesus claims our love.

2 There's not a hope with comfort fraught,
  Triumphant over death and time,
  But Jesus mingles in that thought,
  Forerunner of our course sublime!

3 We see him in the daily round,
  Of social duty, mild and meek,
  With him we tread the hallow'd ground,
  Communion with our God to seek.

4 We see his pitying, gentle eye,
  When lonely want appeals for aid;
  We hear him in the frequent sigh,
  That mourns the waste which sin has made.

5 We meet him at the lowly tomb;
  We weep where Jesus wept before;
  And there, above the grave's dark gloom,
  We see him rise, and weep no more.

SONG 177.—8's & 7's.

1 FROM the table now retiring.
  Which for us the Lord hath spread,
  May our souls, refreshment finding,
  Grow in all things like our Head.

2 His example by beholding,
   May our lives his image bear;
His our Lord and Master calling,
   His commands may we revere.

3 Love to God and man displaying,
   Walking steadfast in thy way,—
Joy attend us in believing,
   Peace from God through endless day.

SONG 178.—L. M.

1 Thy broken body, gracious Lord!
   Is shadow'd by this broken bread;
The wine which in this cup is pour'd,
   Points to the blood which thou hast shed.

2 And while we meet together thus,
   We show that we are one in thee:
Thy precious blood was shed for us,
   Thy death, O Lord, has set us free.

3 We have one hope—that thou wilt come:
   Thee in the air we wait to see:
When thou wilt give thy saints a home,
   And we shall ever reign with thee.

SONG 179.—L. M.

1 Soft be the gentle breathing notes,
   That sings the Savior's dying love;
Soft as the evening zephyr floats,
   Soft as the tuneful lyres above.

2 Soft as the morning dews descend,
   While the sweet lark exulting soars;
So soft to your Almighty Friend,
   Be ev'ry sigh your bosom pours.

3 Pure as the sun's enliv'ning ray,
    That scatters life and joy abroad;
  Pure as the lucid car of day,
    That wide proclaims its Maker, God.

4 True as the magnet to the pole,
    So true let your contrition be—
  So true let all your sorrows roll,
    To him who bled upon the tree.

SONG 180.—L. M.

1 When I survey the wondrous cross
  On which the Prince of glory died,
  All other gain I count but loss,
  And for him give up all beside.

2 See, from his head, his hands, his feet,
  Sorrow and love flow mingled down;
  Did e'er such love and sorrow meet,
  Or thorns compose so rich a crown?

3 Since I, who was undone and lost,
  Have pardon through his name and word;
  Forbid it, then, that I should boast,
  Save in the cross of Christ my Lord.

SONG 181.—8's & 7's.

1. When around us life is shining,
    Touch'd by pleasure's flowing hand,
  When its joys are softly twining
    Round our hearts their silver band:
  When some rich and valued blessing,
    Comes upon each zephyr breath,
  When each wished-for good possessing,
    Oh 'tis hard to think of death.

DEATH.

2 But there's something which can lighten
  All the sorrows of the tomb,
All its dark recesses brighten,
  Dissipate its saddest gloom.
Shed around it beams of glory,
  Bid its every terror flee,
Fill the soul with rapture holy,
  Jesus, 'tis one smile from thee.

SONG 182.—L. M.

1 "Asleep in Jesus!" blessed sleep,
From which none ever wakes to weep :
A calm and undisturb'd repose,
Unbroken by the last of foes.

2 "Asleep in Jesus!" oh how sweet,
To be for such a slumber meet!
With holy confidence to sing,
That death has lost his venom'd sting.

3 "Asleep in Jesus!" peaceful rest,
Whose waking is supremely blest;
Nor fear nor woe shall dim the hour,
That manifests the Savior's power.

4 "Asleep in Jesus!" oh for me
May such a blissful refuge be ;
Securely shall my ashes lie,
And wait the summons from on high.

SONG 183.—C. M.

1 Behold the western evening light !
  It melts in deep'ning gloom,
So calmly Christians sink away,
  Descending to the tomb.

DEATH. 267

2 The winds breathe low; the yellow leaf
   Scarce whispers from the tree;
So gently flows the parting breath,
   When good men cease to be.

3 How beautiful, on all the hills,
   The crimson light is shed:
'Tis like the peace the Christian gives
   To mourners round his bed.

4 How mildly on the wand'ring cloud
   The sunset beam is cast;
So sweet the mem'ry left behind,
   When loved ones breathe their last.

5 And lo! above the dews of night
   The vesper star appears;
So faith lights up the mourner's heart,
   Whose eyes are dim with tears.

6 Night falls, but soon the morning light
   Its glories shall restore;
And thus the eyes that sleep in death
   Shall wake to close no more.

SONG 184.—L. M.

1 JERUSALEM! my glorious home!
   Name ever dear to me!
When shall my labors have an end
   In joy, and peace, and thee?

2 When shall these eyes thy heaven-built walls
   And pearly gates behold?
Thy bulwarks, with salvation strong,
   And streets of shining gold?

3 There happier bowers than Eden's bloom,
   Nor sin nor sorrow know:

DEATH.

Blest seats! through rude and stormy scenes
I onward press to you.

4 Why should I shrink at pain or woe?
Or feel at death dismay?
I've Canaan's goodly land in view,
And realms of endless day.

5 Apostles, martyrs, prophets, there,
Shall round my Savior stand;
Then all my friends in Christ below
Will join the glorious band.

6 Jerusalem! my glorious home!
My soul still pants for thee!
Then shall my labors have an end,
When I thy joys shall see.

SONG 185.—C. M.

1 How long shall death the tyrant reign,
And triumph o'er the just;
While the rich blood of martyrs slain
Lies mingled with the dust?

2 When shall the tedious night be gone?
When will our Lord appear?
Our fond desires would pray him down,
Our love embrace him here.

3 Let faith arise and climb the hills,
And from afar descry
How distant are his chariot wheels,
And tell how fast they fly.

4 We hear the voice, "Ye dead, arise!"
And lo! the graves obey;
And waking saints, with joyful eyes,
Salute th' expected day.

5 How shall our joy and wonder rise,
   When our returning King,
 We'll meet descending through the skies,
   On love's triumphant wing!

SONG 186.—S. M.

1 In expectation sweet,
   We'll wait, and sing, and pray,
 Till Christ's triumphal car we meet,
   And see an endless day.

2 He comes! the Conq'ror comes!
   Death falls beneath his sword:
 The joyful pris'ners burst the tombs,
   And rise to meet their Lord.

3 The trumpet sounds, "Awake!
   Ye dead, to judgment come!"
 The pillars of creation shake,
   While man receives his doom.

4 Thrice happy morn for those
   Who love the ways of peace;
 No night of sorrow e'er shall close,
   Or shade their perfect bliss.

SONG 187.—C. M.

1 There is a house not made with hands,
   Eternal and on high,
 And faith assures I shall possess
   This building, though I die.

2 This earthly house in which I dwell,
   Must speedily decay,
 And in its fall my conscious self
   Must also pass away.

3 But on the resurrection morn,
    My Savior from the skies
Shall come to build anew my form,
    And bid myself arise.

4 While in this earthly house we dwell,
    We share its destiny,
We're absent from the Lord our life,—
    From immortality.

5 For while the body is our home,
    Our life is in its breath;
We live with it, and when it dies
    We perish in its death.

6 Soon shall our house not made with hands,
    Appear at Jesus' word,
When from the flesh we shall be free,
    And present with the Lord.

SONG 188.—8's & 7's, 6 l.

1 Hark! the Archangel's trump is sounding,
    Solemn tones break on the ear;
Louder now, its echoes bounding,
    All the earth astonish'd hear;
        Hallelujah! Hallelujah!
Now Immanuel comes to reign!

2 See the righteous dead are waking.
    Coming forth from dust anew;
Light resplendent o'er them breaking
    Jesus Christ appears to view;
        Hallelujah! Hallelujah!
They arise no more to die.

3 Now the happy throng in union,
    Rise to meet their coming King;

Joyfully they hold communion,
  And their great deliv'rance sing,
  Hallelujah! Hallelujah!
  Ever with the Lord to reign.

SONG 189.—C. M.

1 In hope, against all human hope,
  I can, I do believe;
  Thy quick'ning word shall raise me up,
  With thee, with thee to live.

2 The thing surpasses all my thought;
  But faithful is the Lord;
  Through unbelief, I stagger not,
  For God hath spoke the word.

3 Faith, mighty faith, the promise sees,
  And looks to that alone;
  Laughs at impossibilities,
  And cries, " It shall be done!"

4 To thee, the glory of thy power
  And faithfulness I give!
  I shall from Christ, in that glad hour,
  Eternal life receive.

SONG 190.— P. M.

1 Behold the Lord of glory dies!
  Behold him from the dead arise!
  Redemption is obtain'd:
  Tho' we like him shall yield our breath,
  Like him we soon shall rise from death;
  The vict'ry Christ has gain'd.

2 Why should we fear the gloomy grave?
  Since he, who died our souls to save,
  Will raise our bodies too;

What tho' our earthly house must fail?
The power of Jesus shall prevail,
  To build us up anew.

3 Redeemed! let us his praises sound,
And always in his work abound,
  It shall not be in vain:
A kingdom by our Lord prepared,
And crowns of life, our rich reward,
  And we with him shall reign.

SONG 191.—S. M.

1 Welcome, sweet day of rest,
    That saw the Lord arise!
  Welcome to this reviving breast,
    And these rejoicing eyes!

2 The King himself comes near,
    And feasts his saints to-day;
  Here we may sit, and see him here,
    And love, and praise, and pray.

3 One day in such a place,
    Where thou, my Lord, art seen,
  Is sweeter than ten thousand days
    Of pleasurable sin.

SONG 192.—C. M.

1 Again the Lord of life and light
    Awakes the kindling ray;
  Dispels the darkness of the night,
    And pours increasing day.

2 Oh! what a night was that, which wrapt
    A sinful world in gloom!—
  Oh! what a Sun, which broke, this day,
    Triumphant from the tomb!

3 This day be grateful homage paid,
And loud hosannas sung;
Let gladness dwell in ev'ry heart,
And praise on ev'ry tongue.

SONG 193—L. M.

1 O God, our helper, ever near!
Crown with thy smile the present year.
Preserve us by thy favor still,
And fit us for thy sacred will.

2 Our safety, each succeeding hour,
Depends on thy supporting power.
Accept our thanks for mercies past,
And be our guard while life shall last.

3 Let us not murmur nor complain,
At what thy wisdom shall ordain.
Sickness or health may blessings prove,
As order'd by thy sov'reign love.

4 Our moments move with winged haste,
Nor know we which shall be the last:
Danger and death are ever nigh,
And we this year, perhaps may die.

5 Prepare us for the trying day;
Then shall we meet without dismay,
If thou shalt will, the mortal hour,
Trusting in Christ's reviving power.

SONG 194.—P. M.

1 Sing a loud, a joyful anthem,
Wake earth's purest minstrelsy,

Let it sound from hill to valley,
  And be echoed through the sky:
    Loud thanksgiving
To the God who rules on high:

2 Praises for the radiant sunshine,
    For the dew and genial shower,
  For the soft and cooling zephyr,
    Brought in summer's golden hour:
      Richly freighted,
  When the storm hath spent its power.

3 Praise for health, that priceless treasure,
    Health of body and of mind:
  For the free unbounded pleasure—
    Joys exalted and refined,
      Lavished on us
  By a God supremely kind.

4 For the choice, unnumber'd blessings
    Sent from heaven day by day;
  Food and raiment, peace and friendship,
    Making glad our devious way:
      Let us praise him
  In an humble, fervent lay.

5 More than all, for hope unfading,
    Plant of high celestial birth,
  That hath shed its fragrant blossoms
    O'er this wilderness of earth;
      Life imparting
  Where sin brought its fearful dearth.

6 Sing ye praises! Sing ye praises!
    To the God of truth and love:

Let earth's Jubilee resounding,
  Mingle with the one above!
In thanksgiving
Let each heart with rapture move.

SONG 195.—L. M.

O BLEST Creator of the light!
  Who dost the dawn from darkness bring;
And framing Nature's depth and height,
  Didst with the new-born light begin:

Who gently blending eve with morn,
  And morn with eve, didst call them day:
Thick flows the flood of darkness down;
  Oh, hear us as we humbly pray!

Keep thou our souls from schemes of crime;
  Nor guilt remorseful let them know;
Nor, thinking but on things of time,
  Into eternal darkness go.

Teach us to knock at heaven's high door;
  Teach us the prize of life to win;
Teach us all evil to abhor,
  And purify ourselves within.

SONG 196.—L. M.

1 Now doth the sun ascend the sky,
  And wake creation with its ray;
Keep us from sin, O Lord, most high!
  Through all the actions of the day.

2 Curb Thou for us th' unruly tongue;
  Teach us the way of peace to prize;
And close our eyes against the throng
  Of earth's absorbing vanities.

3 Oh, may our hearts be pure within!
    Nor cherish'd madness vex the soul!
May abstinence the flesh restrain,
    And its rebellious pride control.

4 So when the evening stars appear,
    And in their train the darkness bring;
May we, O Lord, with conscience clear,
    Our praise to thy pure glory sing.

SONG 197.—L. M.

1 LORD of eternal truth and might!
    Ruler of nature's changing scene!
Who dost bring forth the morning light,
    And temper noon's effulgent beam:

2 Quench Thou in us the flames of strife,
    And bid the heat of passion cease;
From perils guard our feeble life,
    And keep our souls in perfect peace.

SONG 198.—L. M.

1 LORD of eternal purity!
    Who dost the world with light adorn,
And paint the tracts of azure sky
    With lovely hues of eve and morn:

2 Who didst command the sun to light
    His fiery wheel's effulgent blaze;
Didst set the moon her circuit bright;
    The stars their ever-winding maze;

3 That, each within its order'd sphere,
    They might divide the night from day;
And of the seasons through the year,
    The well remember'd signs display:

4 Scatter our night, eternal God,
   And kindle thy pure beam within;
 Free us from guilt's oppressive load,
   And break the deadly bonds of sin.

SONG 199.—S. M.

1 " My times are in thy hand,"
   My God, I'd have them there;
 My life, my friends, my soul, I leave
   Entirely to thy care.

2 " My times are in thy hand,"
   Whatever they may be;
 Pleasing or painful, dark or bright,
   As best may seem to Thee.

3 " My times are in thy hand,"
   Why should I doubt or fear?
 My Father's hand will never cause
   His child a needless tear.

4 " My times are in thy hand,"
   I'll always trust in Thee:
 And after death, at thy right hand
   I shall for ever be.

SONG 200.—C. M.

1 O now I long to see that day,
   When the redeem'd shall come
 To Zion, clad in bright array,
   Their blissful, happy home.

2 To hear the alleluias roll
   From the unnumber'd throng:
 The kingdom spread from pole to pole;
   And join redemption's song;

3 To see all Israel safe at home,
 Singing in Zion's height;
And Jesus crown'd upon his throne;
 Creation own his right.

4 All hail! the morn of glory 's nigh,
 The pilgrim longs to see,
That dries the tear from ev'ry eye—
 Creation's Jubilee!

5 Jerusalem I long to see,
 Blest city of my King!
And eat the fruit of Life's fair tree,
 And hear the blood-wash'd sing!

6 My longing heart cries out; O come,
 Creation groans for thee!
The weary pilgrim sighs—O come!
 Bring immortality!

SONG 201.—7's.

1 They who seek the throne of grace,
Find that throne in ev'ry place;
If we live a life of prayer,
God is present ev'rywhere.

2 In our sickness or our health,
In our want or in our wealth,
If we look to God in pray'r,
God is present ev'rywhere.

3 When our earthly comforts fail,
When the foes of life prevail,
'T is the time for earnest pray'r;—
God is present ev'rywhere.

4 Then, my soul, in ev'ry strait
To thy Father come and wait;

He will answer ev'ry pray'r,
God is present ev'rywhere.

SONG 202.—C. M.

1 Since all the coming scenes of time
  God's watchful eye surveys,
O who so wise to choose our lot,
  And regulate our ways?

2 Since none can doubt his equal love,
  Immeasurably kind,
To his unerring gracious will,
  Be ev'ry wish resign'd.

3 Good when He gives, supremely good,
  Nor less when He denies;
E'en crosses from his sov'reign hand,
  Are blessings in disguise.

SONG 203.—P. M.

1 Our Father, high above,
  Look on us in Thy love,
    Oh hear our prayer!
  All hallow'd be Thy Name,
  For holy is the same:
  To spread abroad its fame
    Be our great care.

2 Our hearts with longing wait
  For th' Eternal State,—
    Thy Kingdom come!
  And our petitions rise
  That, as in yonder skies,
  The earth may see likewise
    Thy will be done!

3 We ask for daily bread:
  And let our minds be fed
    From thy rich store!
Oh, let us not be tried
More than the strength supplied:
Free us from ill—and guide
    Us evermore!

4 The Empire—with its might;
  The Glory—ever bright—
    They all are thine!
May we the Kingdom share,
Thou dost for us prepare,
Reign with our Brother there,
    Father divine.

SONG 204.—C. M.

1 THERE is an hour of peaceful rest,
    To lowly wand'rer's given,
  There is joy for those distress'd,
  A balm for every wounded breast.
    A realm as pure as heaven.

2 There is a soft, a downy bed,
    As fair as breath of even;
  A couch for weary mortals spread,
  Where they may rest the aching head,
    Beneath the smiles of heaven.

3 There is a home for weary souls,
    By sin and sorrow driven;
  When toss'd on life's tempestuous shoals,
  When storms arise and ocean rolls
    And all is drear but heaven.

INDEX OF SUBJECTS.

The *Psalms* extend from the 5th to the 83rd page. The Hymns and Songs are arranged as follows:—

HYMNS.

	From Page
Praise to God for Creation	84 to 101
" " Providential favors	102—111
" " the Scriptures	112—123
" " Redemption	124—142

SONGS.

Messiah—Birth	143—147
" Mission	148—154
" Sufferings and Death	155—160
" Resurrection and Ascension	161—172
" Intercession	173—175
" Coming and Reign	176—192
" Kingdom	193—197
Restoration of Israel and Age to come	198—221
Waiting for the Messiah	222—229
Christian Faith	230—233
" Hope	234—237
" Love	238—243
" Holiness	244—245
" Warfare	246—249
" Pilgrimage	250—253
Ordinances—Immersion	254—257
" Supper	258—265
Death	266—268
Resurrection	269—271
Miscellaneous	272—280

INDEX OF FIRST LINES.

First line	Page		First line	Page
Above—below—where	97		Be thou exalted, O my	29
According to thy graci	259		Beyond where Kedron's	156
Again the Lord of life	272		Blest are the souls that	47
A little while our Lord	223		Blest be the everlasting	237
All-powerful, self-exist	94		Blest be the Father of	171
All ye nations, praise	66		Blest be the Lord, who	166
Almighty God, through	135		Blest be the tie that bind	240
Almighty Ruler of the	8		Blest be thy name, O	67
Along the banks where	76		Blow ye the trumpet,	204
Am I a soldier of the cr	245		Bright as the sun's mer	195
Amid the splendors of	139		Bright the vision that	91
Among the princes,	45		Broad is the road that	250
And is the gospel peace	244		Buried with Christ! yes,	256
Asleep in Jesus! blessed	266		But who shall see the	210
As pants the hart for	26		Calm on the list'ning ear	144
At God's command the	32		Children of the heaven	263
Attend, O earth, whilst	8		Christ, the Lord, is risen	162
Awake, my soul! lift up	247		Christian soldier, seize	247
Awake, my soul! stretch	249		Come Jesus, King of Ki	198
Awake, my tongue! thy	99		Come let us raise a joyful	136
Awake, ye saints, and	224		Come, O my soul, in sa	84
Before Jehovah's awful	57		Could I with elocution	136
Begin, my soul, th' exalt	100		Daughter of Zion! awa	210
Begin, my tongue, some	126		Daughter of Zion! from	204
Begin the high, celestial	98		Day of Judgment, day	189
Behold, how joyous in	74		Did Jesus weep? did he	243
Behold, salvation in the	138		Early, my God, without	30
Behold, the bright morn	170		Eternal Power! whose	85
Behold the Lord of glory	271		Eternal source of every	108
"Behold the Man,"	157		Eternal Wisdom, thee	85
Behold! the mountain	209			
Behold the Prince of	149		Faithful, O Lord, thy	129
Behold the Savior of	157		Faithful saints, behold	177
Behold the sure founda	67		Faith, hope, and charity,	239
Behold the western eve	266		Faith, hope, and love,	238
Behold what wondrous	236		Faith is the Christian's	233
Behold where, in a mor	155		Far as the boundless sky	23
Believers, shout and sing	167		"Father divine! the Sa	156

INDEX OF FIRST LINES.

	Page.		Page.
Father, how wide thy	130	Great is the Lord; his	63
Father of mercies, in thy	113	Guide us, O thou great	250
Father, 'tis thine each	107	Had I the tongues of Gr	242
Father! we sing thy	35	Hail, blessed time of end	190
For him who did salva	129	Hail, glorious day, ere	227
From all that dwell be	66	Hail to the brightness of	211
From lowest depths of	72	Hail to the Lord's Anoi	38
From sea to sea, the Ki	196	Happy is he that fears	64
From the recesses of a	111	Happy the heart where	239
From the table now reti	263	Hark! th' archangel's	270
Gird on thy sword, illus	192	Hark, the glad sound!	143
Give glory to God in the	19	Hark! the song of Jubi	194
Give, Lord, the King,	39	Hark! what mean those	144
Give thanks to God most	141	Hasten, Lord, the glori	38
Give to the Lord, ye tri	53	He dies! the friend of	160
Glorious things of thee	45	He lives! the great Re	174
Glory be to God on high!	137	Here, in the broken bre	258
Glory to God and peace	124	He who once was dead,	167
God grant us blessings,	34	High in the heavens,	22
God, in the gospel of his	119	High o'er the heaven of	207
God, in the high and	104	His kingdom comes! ye	194
God is our refuge in dis	27	Hosanna to the Prince	165
God of all created won	88	How are thy servants	61
God of mercy! God of	135	How blest the sacred tie,	240
God of salvation, we ad	25	How calm and beautiful	162
God of the rolling year,	109	How great thy goodness,	19
"Go, preach the Gos	257	How happy are the little	228
Gracious Father, guard	225	How long oh God, shall	40
Grant me within thy	18	How long shall death,	268
Great God, attend, while	42	How long shall that bri	224
Great God! at thy com	105	How many are thy thou	25
Great God, how infinite	94	How oft have sin and	127
Great God! in vain man	96	How precious is thy	117
Great God, indulge my	31	How shall the young se	69
Great God of wonders,	128	How strong thine arm	152
Great God! wert thou	132	How sweet, how heaven	241
Great God, we sing that	108	How sweetly flow'd the	154
Great God! whose uni	36	How wondrous is the	238
Great God, with wonder	116	If human kindness meets	257

INDEX OF FIRST LINES.

	Page.		Page.
If love, the noblest, pur	263	Lo! he comes, with clou	183
I know that my Redeem	233	Lo, he cometh! countles	187
I 'll praise my Maker	79	Lo! Jesus comes with	181
I love the volume of thy	118	Long as the rolling yea	69
Immortal God, on thee	132	Long on the bending wi	202
In blessed union here	261	Look up, ye saints, dire	87
In Jordan's tide the Ba	153	Lo! what an entertain	242
In expectation sweet,	269	Lord, forever at thy side	72
In Judah God of old was	41	Lord, for thy servant	73
In hope, against all hu	270	Lord, I have made thy	70
In many strange and	217	Lord, in the morning th	6
In mem'ry of our absent	260	Lord Jesus, come! for	222
In the cross of Christ I	262	Lord, let my prayer like	77
I sing the almighty pow	102	Lord of eternal purity	276
Isles of the deep rejoice	219	Lord of eternal truth	276
Is there on earth a no	151	Lord of the world's ma	101
I waited meekly for the	24	Lord, our Lord, how gr	7
Jehovah reigns, he dwel	95	Lord, shall the wicked	9
Jehovah reigns, his thr	92	Lord, when iniquities	232
Jerusalem! Jerusalem!	218	Lord, thou hast search'd	76
Jerusalem! my glorious	267	Lord, 't is a pleasant th	49
Jesus, my king, proclai	246	Lord, when thy vine in	42
Jesus, our Lord, ascend	63	Lord, who's the happy	11
Jesus shall reign where	37	May ev'ry year draw	221
Jesus! the friend of	261	'Mid scenes of confusion	253
Jesus will come to earth	212	Morning breaks upon	161
Jesus will come—the	177	Much in sorrow, oft in	248
Joy cometh! O! when	176	My blest Redeemer and	244
Joy to the world, Mes	55	My God, My King, thy	78
Kingdoms and thrones	35	My helper, God! I bless	107
Know, my soul, thy full	235	My song of praise, O	15
Laden with guilt and full	123	My soul is happy when	226
Let all on earth their voi	89	My soul repeat his prai	59
Let all the heathen writ	121	My soul, thy great Cre	60
Let God arise in all his	34	"My times are in thy	277
Let others boast of weal	121	Nor King nor prince on	200
Let Zion and her sons	58	Not to ourselves, who	65
Lift up your heads in	146	Not with terror do we	259
Lift your glad voices in	169	Now be my heart inspir	26

INDEX OF FIRST LINES. 285

	Page.		Page.
Now doth the sun ascend	275	Praise him with a loud	65
Now let our humble fai	173	Praise the Lord, his po	82
Now pray we for Jerusa	215	Praise the Lord, ye hea	92
Now to the Lord a noble	125	Praise to God, immortal	110
O all ye nations, clap	28	Praise to Him, by whos	120
O blest Creator of the	275	Praise to thee, thou gr	80
O boundless goodness!	139	Praise ye the Lord—my	78
O come, loud anthems	51	Praise ye the Lord! 'tis	96
O come let us sing to	52	Praise ye the Lord! yet	81
O glorious hope of hea	234	Prophetic era! blissful	186
O God, all-holy, good,	138	Raise your triumphant	137
O glorious hour! when	193	Rejoice in the Lord, O	21
O God, my heart is full	62	Rejoice, ye righteous,	20
O God, on thee we all	106	Rise, crown'd with ligh	202
O God, our helper ever	273	Sacred and true, O righ	68
O God, our help in ages	48	See from on high a light	148
Oh! give us, Lord, thy	44	Shine, mighty God, on	32
Oh praise the Lord with	74	Shout for the blessed Je	220
Oh, pray for Salem's	71	Since all the coming see	279
O how I long to see that	277	Sing a loud, and joyful	237
O Lord, how just and	59	Sing praise, the tomb is	164
O Lord of hosts, my Ki	43	Sing to the Lord, ye	53
O Lord our heavenly	90	Sing the redeemed of	251
O love divine! what hast	160	Soft be the gentle brea	264
On the mountain's top	215	So let our lips and lives	245
On Zion's mount, as pro	217	Songs of immortal prais	133
O praise ye the Lord pre	81	Songs of praise the an	163
O render thanks to God	61	Soon as I heard my fath	17
O, speed thee, Christian	249	Soon righteousness shall	197
O thou fount of ev'ry	131	Sweet is the memory of	140
O thou, my light, my lif	103	Sweet is the work, my	49
Our country is Immanu	251	That glorious day is	198
Our Father, high above	279	The Almighty reigns,	54
Our Father, high enthr	190	The Church has waited	229
Our Lord is risen from	16	The earth shall rejoice	111
Our Savior Christ will	185	The followers about our	197
Our Savior lives, no mor	169	The heavens declare thy	114
O worship the King all	88	The lands that long in	147
Praise for the book of	112	The last lovely morning	183

INDEX OF FIRST LINES.

First Line	Page	First Line	Page
The law by Moses came	148	Thy law is perfect, Lord	14
The Lord before me still	11	Thy name, Almighty Lo	142
The Lord is coming in	176	Thy people, Lord, who	191
The Lord is coming, let	182	Thy word, O Lord, is li	115
The Lord is in his holy	10	Thy years, O Lord, are	57
The Lord is King, enthr	56	'T is by the faith of joys	230
The Lord is King in	50	'T is faith that purifies	232
The Lord my Shepherd	105	'T is finish'd! so the Sa	159
The Lord our God is	86	To bless thy chosen race	33
The Lord will come, the	188	To our almighty Maker,	55
The morn is breaking	201	To God, loud hallelujahs	80
The night is far spent	182	To thee, O Lord, I raise	9
The night is wearing fa	180	To thy pastures fair and	16
The people of the Lord	252	To wait for that predict	221
The race that long in	147	Triumphant, Christ asc	172
There is an hour of pea	280	Triumphant Zion, lift thy he	199
The sands of time are	208	'T was by an order from the	118
The Savior comes his ad	180	'T was the commission of	254
The spacious firmament	12	'T was the day when God's	158
The trump of God shall	192	Unto our God, on Judahs hills	206
The true Messiah now	152	Welcome sight, the Lord descen	184
There is a hope, a bless	235	Welcome, sweet day of rest,	272
		What a mercy, what a treasure,	122
They who seek the thr	278	What works of wisdom, power,	150
Thine oath and promise	231	What glory gilds the sacred pag	120
		When around us life is shining,	265
This age is speedily to	219	When gathering clouds around	175
This shall be the people	83	When God descends with men	200
		When God fulfils his promised	211
Thou art, O God, the	93	When in silence o'er the deep	124
Thou God, before whose	46	When I the holy grave survey	171
		When I survey the wondrous cr	265
Thou hast said, exalted	255	When overwhelmed with grief	80
Thou hast, O God, pro	134	When the King of Kings comes	179
Thou, who art enthron	101	While shepherds watch'd their	145
		Who trust the Lord's almighty	71
Though we know not of	223	With all my powers of heart and	117
Thrice happy he who	5	With glory clad, with strength	50
		With my whole heart I've soug	116
Throned on a cloud our	29	With joy we meditate the grace,	172
Throned on a cloud the	189	Ye humble souls, approach your	141
Through all the chang	22	Ye humble souls, that seek the	164
		Ye people of Israel, remember	216
Through ev'ry age, eter	47	Ye servants of the Lord,	226
Thy broken body, grac	264	Yes, Judah's harp shall sound	203
		Ye who rise to meet the Lord	228
Thy favors, Lord, surpr	127	Zion arise, put on thy strength	214
Thy goodness, Lord, our	126	Zion's King shall reign victorio	206

SCRIPTURAL INDEX.

PART. I—PSALMS.

No.	Psa.	No.	Psa.	No.	Psa.	No.	Psa.
1	i.	30	xlii	59	lxxxix.	88	cxv.
2	ii.	31	xlv.	60	"	89	cxvii.
3	v.	32	xlvi.	61	xc.	90	"
4	viii.	33	xlvii.	62	"	91	cxviii.
5	"	34	l.	63	xcii.	92	cxix.
6	ix.	35	lvii.	64	"	93	"
7	x.	36	lxi.	65	xciii.	94	"
8	xi.	37	lxiii.	66	"	95	"
9	xv.	38	"	67	xcv.	96	"
10	xvi.	39	lxv.	68	"	97	cxxii.
11	xix.	40	lxvii.	69	xciv.	98	cxxv.
12	"	41	"	70	xcvi.	99	cxxx.
13	"	42	"	71	xcvii.	100	cxxxi.
14	xxii.	43	lxviii.	72	xcviii.	101	cxxxii.
15	xxiii.	44	"	73	"	102	cxxxiii.
16	"	45	"	74	xcix.	103	cxxxv.
17	xxiv.	46	lxxii.	75	c.	104	cxxxvi.
18	xxvii.	47	"	76	cii.	105	cxxxvii.
19	"	48	"	77	"	106	cxxxix.
20	xxix.	49	"	78	ciii.	107	cxli.
21	xxxi.	50	"	79	"	108	cxlv.
22	xxxii.	51	lxxiv.	80	civ.	109	cxlvi.
23	xxxiii.	52	lxxvi.	81	cv.	110	"
24	xxxiv.	53	lxxx.	82	cvii.	111	cxlvii.
25	xxxvi.	54	lxxxiv.	83	cviii.	112	"
26	"	55	"	84	cx.	113	"
27	xl.	56	lxxxv.	85	cxi.	114	cxlix.
28	"	57	lxxxvi.	86	cxii.	115	cl.
	"	58	lxxxvii.	87	cxiii.	116	cxlviii.

HYMNS.—PART II.

Book & Chap.	No.	Book & Chap.	No.	Book & Chap.	No.
GENESIS.		xxiii.	30	Isa. vi.	10
i.	5, 57	xciii.	16	Micah vii. 18	64
1 SAMUEL.		cxix.	44	LUKE.	
vii. 12	32, 68	" 96	53	ii. 9–14	57, 58
PSALMS.		cxxxviii.	47	JOHN.	
viii.	9	cxlvii. 1–5	18	iii. 16, 17	77
xix.	42, 49	cxlviii.	12	1 Pet. i.	21

SONGS.—PART III.

PSALMS.		MARK.		2 COR.	
xxxi. 15	199	i. 4–11	15	v. 1–4	187
xlv. 4–6	71	xiv. 36	20	GALATIANS.	
lxxii.	76	xvi. 1–6	29	v. 6.	126
xcvii.	78	" 15, 16	167	vi. 14.	180
ISAIAH.		LUKE.		EPHESIANS.	
ii. 2–4	72, 94	ii. 9–14	2, 3, 4	vi. 12–18	180
" 10–22	73	iv. 18, 19,	1	1 THESS.	
ix. 1–6	6, 7	xii. 35, 37	119	iv. 16	49, 188
xxv.	95	" " "	122	HEBREWS.	
lii.	100	xxii. 19	172	iii. 3, 5, 6	9
lx.	99	JOHN.		iv. 15, 16	43
Hos. iii. 4, 5	82	i. 17.	9	x. 28, 29	9
ZECHARIAH.		xi. 35	17	xii. 1, 2	155
xiv. 4, 5	64	xix. 5	21	1 PETER.	
MATTHEW.		" 30	22, 24	i. 3–5	41, 135
iii. 16, 17	8	ROMANS.		1 JOHN.	
vi. 9–13	68, 199	vi. 4.	166	iii. 1–3	132, 136
xxvi. 36–44	19	1 COR.		REVELATION.	
xxvii. 45	23	xi. 24, 25	168	vii. 9–17	67
xxviii. 1	27, 28	xiii.	138	xi. 17, 18	70
" 19	163	"	144, 145	xix. 6	74

www.ingramcontent.com/pod-product-compliance
Lightning Source LLC
Chambersburg PA
CBHW052214240426
43670CB00037B/441